Handl

# Philippian Studies in Faith and Love from St. Paul's Epistle to the Philippians

outlook

Handley C.G Moule

# Philippian Studies Lessons in Faith and Love from St. Paul's Epistle to the Philippians

1st Edition | ISBN: 978-3-75241-201-7

Place of Publication: Frankfurt am Main, Germany

Year of Publication: 2020

Outlook Verlag GmbH, Germany.

Reproduction of the original.

# PHILIPPIAN STUDIES

Lessons in Faith and Love from
St. Paul's Epistle to the Philippians

by

H. C. G. MOULE, D.D.

1

# PREFACE

The plan and purpose of the following pages will be soon evident to the reader. The whole aim is towards edification. What is said in the way of historical introduction, what is done in the course of the chapters in the way of rendering and grammatical explanation, all has this aim in view. The Epistle is handled throughout with the firm belief that it is an Oracle of God, while that Oracle is conveyed through the mind and heart of one of the greatest of the sons of men; and the Expositor's aim accordingly is always, and above all things, to expound. To put it otherwise, his highest ambition is to call attention to the sacred text, and let it speak.

May the Lord of the Apostle, of the Philippians, of ourselves, only grant that His mercy may rest upon this poor contribution to the exegesis of His inexhaustible Word. May it be permitted to throw a quiet light upon some of the treasures of this apostolic casket, to the help, in any measures, of the disciples of our day. Then will the Expositor indeed give thanks to the Master at whose feet he lays his work.

**RIDLEY HALL, CAMBRIDGE.**

# *INTRODUCTORY*

O Gracious GOD and most mercifull Father, which hast vouchsafed us the rich and precious iewell of thy holy worde, assist us with thy Spirit, that it may be written in our hearts to our euerlasting comfort, to reforme us, to renew us according to thine owne image, to build us up, and edifie us into the perfect building of thy Christ, sanctifying and increasing in us all heauenly vertues. Graunt this O heauenly Father, for Iesus Christes sake. Amen.

*From the* GENEVA BIBLE, 1557.

# CHAPTER I

INTRODUCTORY

Characteristics of the Epistle—The Bible is ever young—Littera Scripta Manet—"This Same Jesus"—Philippi—How the mission church had grown —Where was the Epistle written?—When was the Epistle written?—"The word endureth"

The Epistle of St Paul to the Philippians is, to careful and loving Bible-students, one of the fairest and dearest regions of the Book of God. It is true that the Christian who genuinely believes that "every Scripture is God-inspired" (2 Tim. iii. 16), and who realizes that the "Divine *Library*" is nevertheless, and from a higher point of view, One *Book* all through, will be always on the guard against a mistaken favouritism in his Scripture studies. He will strive to make himself in some sense familiar with the whole Book, *as* a whole, and to recognize in all its parts the true Author's hand and purpose. Yet it is inevitable that in this supreme Book, as in other books, though all parts are "co-operant to an end," all parts are not equally important for the deepest needs of the reader. The reader therefore will have to be more familiar with some parts than with others. Acquaintance with the whole will indeed deepen insight into the part. But it will not supersede our study, loving and special, of the part which, in a degree and manner peculiar to itself, "is able to make us wise unto salvation, through faith which is in Christ Jesus."

The present simple Studies in the Philippian Epistle will accordingly be pursued with the desire to remember as we go the whole scriptural revelation of God and salvation. But we shall also approach the Epistle as a peculiarly precious Scripture in itself, containing in its few short pages a rare fulness of messages and teachings, meeting the inmost wants of the heart and the life.

Amongst the Epistles of St Paul Philippians shines out with singular light and beauty. In such a comparison we scarcely need consider the great Epistles to Rome and Corinth; their large scale and wide variety of topics set them apart. Nor need we consider Hebrews, with its difficult problem of authorship. Looking at the other Epistles, each with its own divine and also deeply human characteristics, we find Philippians more peaceful than Galatians, more personal and affectionate than Ephesians, less anxiously controversial than Colossians, more deliberate and symmetrical than Thessalonians, and of course larger in its applications than the personal messages to Timothy, Titus, and Philemon. Meanwhile it is as comprehensive almost as it is brief. It presents more than one important passage of doctrine, some of these passages being revelations of the first order. It is full of pregnant precepts for Christian character and conduct, whether seen in the individual or in the community. It discloses in a way of the utmost interest and significance the circumstances and experiences of the writer, and also, in a measure, of the readers. And the whole is suffused with a singularly sweet light of "joy and peace in believing." It is written by one who was, as he wrote, at once resting and moving in the peace of God which passes understanding, and in the love of Christ which passes knowledge; and what is felt in his soul comes out inevitably on his page. The letter, written in a prison, and addressed to a mission-church always exposed to insult and assault, yet seems in a wonderful way to call us "apart, to rest awhile." "A glory gilds the sacred page," the glory of the presence of the Lord in all His majesty of Godhead and nearness of Manhood; in His finished work, and living power, and wonderful coming again. A peculiar sort of joy, which is impossible without at least the experience, if not the presence, of sorrow, rests and shines over the whole. It is the joy of the heart which has found at length "the secret of the Lord," His hiding-place from the tyranny of circumstances and time; the way how always to be of good cheer, naturally yet also supernaturally, not by a hard-won indifference to life, but by living, amidst everything external, "hidden with Christ in God."

Let us approach the beloved pages once again. They can never wear out; there will always prove to be "more to follow." Perhaps we have loved and pondered them for long years ourselves. Perhaps we have heard them expounded by voices silent now, "in days that never come again," in chambers or in churches which we seem still to see, but which in fact have passed from us very far away. The heart is full and the eyes are wet as we look back. But the melancholy of the past has no permanent place in Bible-study. The Book is divine, immortal, and ever young. He who was in it for our fathers is in it for us. And since He is in it, as He is in no other literature in the world, (because no other literature is His Word Written,) therefore it springs up to us ever new; it is always contemporary with every generation of believers. Even so, come, Lord Jesus, and let us meet Thee in Thy Scripture now again.

A very simple "Introduction" will suffice for our present purposes. These chapters make no pretension to be, in the technical sense, critical. I say next to nothing, for example, about the Authenticity and Genuineness of the Epistle. Let me only remind the reader that from the early dawn of the literature of the Church we have unmistakable testimonies to its existence as an apostolic Scripture. Ignatius and Polycarp, quite early in the second century, shew us that they have read it. A little later, in the "Epistle of the Churches of Lyons and Vienne" (A.D. 177),[1] it is quoted. Clement of Alexandria, and Irenaeus, and Tertullian, all in the second century, use it as "the sword of the Spirit" to assert truth and confute error. So it floats down into the broad stream of the patristic literature at large. Not till the rise of an ultra-sceptical criticism in quite modern times was Philippians ever seriously questioned as the work, in its integrity, of St Paul. And Baur's objections, all due to an *à priori* theory, not to an impartial literary enquiry, have been repudiated even by critics even less orthodox than himself: Renan, for example. It is quite as certain, in a literary sense, that in Philippians we have the very words and heart of St Paul as that we have Addison in the papers signed C. in the *Spectator*, or Erasmus in the correspondence with Colet.

And what a thought of strength and joy this is to the believer of our latter day! *Littera scripta manet.* How impressive is the permanence of every written reflexion of the mind, and of the life! Who has not felt it, even in the reading of a private letter to himself, written years and years ago? We have St Paul speaking to us in this indelible page as really as if we were seated with him in "his own hired house," and were *listening* as he dictates to the friend beside him. And as we recollect this, we reflect that all he is saying, all he has thus left written, is just so much testimony to the Lord Jesus Christ, contemporary, direct, inspired. When the words we are about to read were written, scarcely thirty years had passed away since the Son of Man died outside the gate of Jerusalem, and rose again. Perhaps my reader cannot look back over thirty years, perhaps not over twenty, with conscious memory. But I can; and beyond the thirty I can see a long vista of the still earlier past. Thirty years ago[2];—at that time the great conflict between Austria and Prussia was preparing, the issue of which was so long a step towards the unification of Germany. I was then a master in a public school. The discussions of the impending war in our common-room, and the men who joined in them, are very present still to my mind; certainly not the faintest haze of mythical change or disproportion has had time to gather over those scenes in the interval. With some differences, no doubt, the world of this day is yet essentially the same as the world of that day; I certainly still, in my whole personal consciousness, am the man of that day, only somewhat developed in experience. Well, what the date of the battle of Sadowa (Königgratz) is to me, such was the date of the Crucifixion to St Paul, when he wrote from Rome to his dear converts at Philippi. And I venture to say that, while St Paul's tone about the Lord of Calvary is of course immeasurably different in the highest respects from what mine might be had I to speak of the makers of European history of 1866, it is in one respect just the same. It is as completely free from the tone of legend unreality, uncertainty. With the same entire consciousness of matter of fact with which I might write of the statesmen or generals of my early manhood, he writes of One who, in *his* early manhood, overcame death by death, and "shewed Himself alive after His passion by many infallible proofs."

Only, there is this wonderful difference; that for St Paul the Jesus Christ of recent history is absolutely One with the Jesus Christ of his present spiritual experience. The Man of the Cross is also, for him, the Lord who is exalted to the throne of heaven, and is also so related to the writer that Paul is "in Christ Jesus," with a proximity and union which enters into everything. "In Him" are included the very actions of the disciple's mind and the experiences of his heart. He is the Lord who lives in the inmost being of His servant, and who yet is also expected to return from the heavens, to transfigure the servant's very body into glory. The Christ of history, the Christ of the soul—it was "this same Jesus" then; it is "this same Jesus" now.

> "Can length of years on God Himself exact,
> Or make that fiction which was once a fact?
> Fix'd in the rolling flood of endless years
> The pillar of the eternal plan appears;
> The raging storm and dashing wave defies,
> Built by that Architect who built the skies." [3]

For me and for my reader may the two aspects of "this same Jesus," the historical and the spiritual, ever combine in one mighty harmony of certainty; faith's resting-place to the end, "the rock of our heart, and our portion for ever"; at once our peace and our power, in life and in death, and through the eternal day also, in which we shall need Him still in the experiences of heaven.

What shall we say of the place to which the Epistle was sent, and of that from which it was written; and of the writer, the bearer, the readers; and of the occasion and the time?

Philippi now, so travellers tell us, is a scene of beautiful and silent ruin. Near the head of the fair Archipelago, amidst scenery of exquisite beauty, near the range of Pangaeus, now Pirnari, on the banks of the quiet Gangas, lie the relics of the once busy city, visited only by the herdsman and the explorer. By it or through it ran a great road from West to East, called by the Romans the Egnatian Way. The double battle of Philippi, B.C. 42, when the Oligarchy fell finally before the rising Empire, made the plain famous. Augustus planted a *colonia* in the town. It thus became a miniature Rome, as every "colony" was. It had its pair of petty consuls (*duumviri*; the *strategoi* of Acts xvi. 20) and their lictors (A.V. "serjeants," *rhabdouchoi*). And it faithfully reproduced Roman pride in the spirit of its military settlers. It had its Jewish element, as almost every place then had; but the Jews must have been few and despised; their place of worship was but a "prayer-house" (*proseuchê*), outside the walls, on the river's bank (Acts xvi. 13). We need not recount in detail the history of the first evangelization (A.D. 52) of the difficult place. We recollect sufficiently the address to the pious Jewesses and proselyte-women in the "prayer-house"; the conversion and baptism of Lydia; the rescue of the poor girl possessed with the "spirit of Pytho"; the tumult, and the trial before the duumvirs; the scourge, the inner prison, the hymn at midnight, the earthquake, and the salvation of the jailor's life and soul; the message sent through the lictors in the morning, then the respectful approach of the magistrates themselves, and the retirement of the Missionaries "to another city," along the Egnatian road. It is enough now to remember, what the very existence of the Epistle reveals to us, the growth and life of the little mission-church planted amidst such storms, and in a climate, so to speak, full of possible tempests at any hour. In the Epistle, we arrive at a date some nine years later than the first visit of St Paul. Twice during that period, and perhaps only twice, we find him at Philippi again; late in A.D. 57 (Acts xx. 1) and early (it was the sweet spring, the Passover time) in A.D. 58; this last may have been a visit arranged on purpose (in Lightfoot's words: *Philippians*, p. 60) "that he might keep the Paschal feast with his beloved converts." No doubt, besides these personal visits, Philippi was kept in contact with its Missionary between A.D. 52 and A.D. 61 by messages and by the occasional visits of the Apostle's faithful helpers. But on the whole the Church would seem in a very large degree to have been left to its own charge. And what do we find as the issue when we come to the Epistle? A community large enough to need a *staff* of Christian ministers, "bishops and deacons," "overseers and working-helpers" (*episkopoi kai diakonoi*); full of love and good works; affectionately mindful of St Paul in the way of practical assistance; and apparently shewing, as their almost only visible defect or danger, a tendency to separate somewhat into sections or cliques—a trouble which in itself indicates a considerable society. If we may (as we may, looking at the ordinary facts of human nature) at all estimate the calibre of Philippian Christianity by the tone in which the Apostle addresses the Philippians, we gather that on the whole it was a high tone, at once decided and tender, affectionate and mature. The converts were capable of responding to a deep doctrinal teaching, and also to the simplest appeals of love. Such was the triumph of the mysterious Gospel over place, and circumstance, and character; the lily flowered at its fairest among the thorns; grace shone and triumphed in the immediate presence of its "adversaries."

But the evil we indicated just above was present in the otherwise happy scene. When Epaphroditus crossed the mountains and the sea to carry a generous gift of money to St Paul, risking his life (ii. 27) somehow by dangerous sickness in the effort, he had to carry also news of differences and heart-burnings, which could not but cloud the Apostle's loving joy. The envoy found it needful to speak also of the emissaries of error who at Philippi, as everywhere, were troubling the faith and hope of the believers; "turning the grace of God into lasciviousness"; professing a lofty spirituality, and worshipping their appetites all the while. And side by side with them, apparently, might be found Pharisaic disputants of an older type (iii. 3, 18, etc.).

Such was the report with which Epaphroditus found his way from Macedonia to Rome. Where, in Rome, did he find St Paul, and at what stage of his Roman residence? Our answer must begin with affirming the conviction that it *was* to Rome, not elsewhere, that Epaphroditus went. The reader is aware that the Epistle itself names no place of origin; it only alludes to a scene of *imprisonment*. And this does not of itself decide the locality; for at Caesarea Stratonis, in Palestine, as well as at Rome, St Paul spent two years in captivity (Acts xxiv. 27). Some modern critics have favoured the date from Caesarea accordingly. They have noticed e.g. the verbal coincidence between Herod's *praetorium* (A.V. "judgment-hall") of Acts xxiii. 35, and the *praetorium* (A.V. "palace") of Phil. i. 13. But Lightfoot[4] seems to me right in his decisive rejection of this theory and unshaken adherence to the date from Rome. He remarks that the oldest Church tradition is all for Rome; that the Epistle itself evidently refers to its place of origin as to a place of first-rate importance and extent, in which any advance of the Gospel was a memorable and pregnant event; and that the allusion to "Caesar's household" (though it is not so quite decisive as it might at first sight appear to be) "cannot without much straining of language and facts be made to apply to Caesarea."

If now the Epistle was written from Rome, during the "two whole years" of Acts xxviii. 30, at what point in that period may we think that the writing fell? Here again is a problem over which much thought and labour has been spent. A majority of opinions no doubt is in favour of a date towards the end of the imprisonment, so that Philippians would follow after Colossians and Ephesians. It is held that (1) the tone of the Epistle betokens the approach of a closing crisis for St Paul; and that (2) it seems to indicate an already developed Christian mission work at Rome, as if St Paul had worked there some while; and that (3) Epaphroditus' visit cannot be adjusted with any probability if we do not allow a good time for previous communications between Rome and Philippi. But here again Lightfoot's view commends itself to my mind decisively. He holds that Philippians was *the first* of the "Epistles of the Captivity," and was written perhaps within the first few months of the "two whole years." Two of his reasons seem adequate of themselves to make this likely. The first is, that St Paul's allusion to the profound *impression made on the Roman Christians* by his "bonds in Christ" (i. 13, 14) goes well with the hypothesis of his recent arrival as a prisoner for Christ's sake, but not

9

with that of his having been long present on the scene. The other is that the great doctrinal passage (iii. 4-9), where he repudiates "his own righteousness" and commits himself to "the righteousness which is of God by faith," is evidently akin to the group of Epistles to which Romans belongs; and that it seems more likely that the divine Inspirer, in His order of revelation, led His servant so to write while the occasion for the writing of Romans was still comparatively recent, than long after, when the different (though kindred) sides of saving truth dealt with in Ephesians and Colossians had become prominent in his teaching. With reason, I think, Lightfoot "cannot attach any weight" to the argument from Epaphroditus' visit, which may well have been planned at Philippi before St Paul actually reached Rome, and planned thus early on purpose, so as to reach him promptly there with the collected gifts of love. Nor are the allusions to a probable impending crisis in the trial before the Emperor important for the date; for quite early in the imprisonment it may well have seemed likely that the case would be soon decided. As for the comparatively advanced state of Roman Christianity, the Epistle to the Romans is evidence enough that a vigorous and extensive mission-church, however it was founded, existed at Rome some years before St Paul arrived.

I will venture then to take it for granted that it was some time in A.D. 61, or at latest early in A.D. 62, that Epaphroditus came, with his collection and his reports, and struggled through his illness, and then prepared to return to Macedonia, carrying this precious Letter with him. We seem to see the scene as he converses day by day with St Paul, and as at length he takes his leave, in charge of this Message of "faith and love." We see a large chamber in one of those huge piles of building, storey over storey, of which imperial Rome was full. The window looks perhaps north-westward, up the stream of the Tiber, towards the distant hills of which Soracte is the most prominent. The sentinel, perhaps himself a convert to the Lord, sits motionless at a little distance, chained to the Apostle. The saints pray, converse, and embrace; and then Epaphroditus descends to set out for Ostia, or for Puteoli, on his way home to Philippi.

"The grass withereth, the flower fadeth, but the Word of the Lord endureth for ever." The graves of the blessed ones who worked for the heavenly Master then are more than eighteen centuries old now. But the Letter to Philippi is to-day as new as ever. It is addressed to us, that we too may "believe, unto life everlasting," on "that same Jesus."

[1] Preserved by Eusebius, *Hist. Eccl.*, ii.

[2] Written early in 1896.

[3] Cowper, *Conversation*.

10

[4] *Philippians* (ed. i.), p. 30, note.

"Man, like the grass of morning,
 Droops ere the evening hour;
His goodliness and beauty
 Fade as a fading flower;
But who may shake the pillars
Of God's unchanging Word?
Amen, Himself hath spoken;
Amen,—thus saith the Lord.
      BISHOP E. H. BICKERSTETH.

# THE INTIMACY OF HUMAN HEARTS IN CHRIST

"I learned without booke almost all Paules Epistles, yea and I weene all the Canonical! Epistles, save only the Apocalyps. Of which study, although in time a great part did depart from me, yet the sweete smell thereof I trust I shall cary with me into heaven."

**BISHOP RIDLEY, 1555.**

# CHAPTER II

## THE INTIMACY OF HUMAN HEARTS IN CHRIST

PHILIPPIANS i. 1-11

The Apostle and his converts one—The possible isolation of hearts—Union with and in Christ—Christ and the personality—Christ the secret of intimacy —Is the secret ours?—Reserve in Christian intercourse

Let us begin our verbal study of the Letter which Epaphroditus carried to Philippi. We attempt first a translation of its first main section, interspersed with an explanatory paraphrase. This will be followed by a brief meditation upon one of the main "Lessons in Faith and Love" suggested by the section.

Ver. 1. +Paul and Timotheus, bondservants of Christ Jesus, to all the holy ones+ in union with +Christ Jesus who are living at Philippi, Overseers, Workers, and all+.[1]

Ver. 2. +Grace to you, and peace+—all the free favour of acceptance and of divine presence, and all the repose which it brings, within you and around you —from God our Father and the Lord Jesus Christ,

Vers. 3, 4. +I give thanks to my God+ (He is mine, as I am His) +over my whole memory of you; always in each request of mine on behalf of you all forming and expressing+ (*poioumenos*[2]) +that+ (*tên*) +request with joy+;

Ver. 5. +on account of your participation with me in regard of the Gospel+, your active co-operation with me, by prayer, by work, by gifts, in the Gospel work,

Ver. 6. +from the first day up to this present. For+ (the thought of your long consistency suggests the assertion) +I am quite sure of just this, that He who inaugurated+ (*enarkamenos*: the word has solemn, ceremonial connexions) +in you the[3] good work will perfect it+, will evermore put His finishing touches to it (*epitelesei*), up to +Christ Jesus' Day+, the Day of His promised Return, and of our glorification with Him. But this is by the way; I return to my joy and my

Ver. 7. thanksgivings over you: +Even as it is just that I+, I above all men (*emoi*, emphatic, not *moi*), +should feel+ (*phronein*) +like this over you all, on behalf of you all,[4] because of my having you in my heart, as those who, alike in my imprisonment+ (*desmois*) +and in the vindication and establishment of the Gospel+, the defence of it against its enemies, the developement of its truths and its power in the believing, +are copartners, all of you, of my grace+; my grace, the grace granted me, the glorious privilege of suffering and of doing as a Missionary of Christ. Your loving, working sympathy has inextricably united you and me, alike in my prison and in my apostolate.

Ver. 8. Yes, I feel this in my inmost being. +For God is my witness, how I yearn+, as with a homesick affection (*epipothia*), +for you all, in the heart+ (*splagchna*) +of Christ Jesus+; for to His members His heart is as it were theirs; our emotions are, by the Spirit, in contact with His.

Ver. 9. +And+ what are those "requests" which I make for you with joy? +This is my prayer, that your love+, in the fullest Christian sense, but above all in the sense of your love to one another, +may abound yet more and more+ in the attendant and protective blessing of +spiritual knowledge+ (*epignôsis*) and all needed

Ver. 10. +discernment; so that+, amidst life's many temptations to compromises of conviction or inconsistency of spirit, +you may test the things that differ+ (*ta diapherona*), sifting truth and holiness from their counterfeits; +in order to be singlehearted+ (*eilikrineis*[5]) +and without a stumbling-block+, such as error and inconsistency so easily lay in our further path, +against+, in view of, +Christ's Day+; so that when that Day dawns you may be found to be not servants whose time has been half lost for their Lord's work and will, but

Ver. 11. rather those +who have been filled with the fruit+ (*karpon*, not *karpôn*) of righteousness—the result, in witness and service, of your reconciliation and renewal,[6] fruit which is borne +through Jesus Christ+, the Procurer and the Secret of your fruit-bearing life, to +God's praise and glory+, the true goal and end of all our blessings and of all our labours.

So the Letter opens; with greeting, with benediction, and then with an outpouring, of sympathies full at once of the warmest and tenderest *humanity* and of the inmost secrets of divine truth and life. It is a preamble beautifully characteristic not only of St Paul but of the Gospel. It illustrates from many sides the happy fact that there is nothing which so effectually opens human hearts to one another as the love of Christ. We are all sadly familiar with the possibilities of isolation between heart and heart. Poets have written with eloquent melancholy of our personalities as islands which lie indeed near together, but in an unfathomable ocean, over whose channels no boat has ever passed. Schools of pessimistic thought have positively affirmed that never really has one *ego* found its way into another through the hermetic seal of individuality; all that we seem to know of others is but the action of our own mind within itself, occasioned by a blind collision with a something not itself, which we can strike upon but can never really know. Such lucubrations are artificial, not natural; a distortion of mysterious facts, not an exposition of them; the result of an arbitrary selection from the data of our consciousness, and then the treatment of the selection as if it were the whole. Quite apart from the Gospel, the facts of human intercourse are full of evidence to wonderful and beautiful possibilities of insight and intercourse between human spirit and spirit. But if we want to read the best possible negative to the gloomy dream of impenetrable isolation, we must come to the Lord Jesus Christ. We must make experiment of what it is, in Him, to know and love others who are in Him too. Then indeed we shall find that we can, in the common possession of a living Lord who dwells in our hearts by faith, see as it were from heart into heart, in the warm light of His presence. We shall find how wonderful is the friendship with one another to which the friends of Jesus are called, and for which they are enabled in Him.

"IN HIM": those words are the key to this deep, tender, healthful union, and as it were fusion, of souls. We have the truth which they convey prominent already in the Philippian Letter. It is addressed (ver. 1) to "the holy ones in Christ Jesus." That is to say, it comes to men and women who, taken on their profession, assumed to be in fact what they were denoted to be in baptism, were separated from self and sin to God by their union in covenant and life with their Redeemer. It regards them as personalities so truly annexed by Jesus Christ, in the miracle of converting grace, so articulated spiritually into Him, that no language short of this wonderful "in Him" will worthily express their relation to Him. Later (ver. 11), they are regarded as so united to Him that "the fruit of righteousness" which they are to bear in rich abundance is to be borne only "*through* Him"; He, the Vine, is the one possible secret by which they, the branches, can possibly be productive of the sweet cluster of "the fruit of the Spirit." And between those two places comes a sentence (ver. 8) where, just in passing, in a mere allusion to his own experience, the Apostle takes for granted this profound "continuity with Christ" in a peculiarly impressive way:

"I long after you all in the heart of Jesus Christ." As we have seen above, he regards himself (not as an Apostle but simply as a believer) as so "joined unto the Lord" that, if I may dare so to expand the phrase, the heart of Jesus Christ is the true organ and vehicle of his own regenerate emotions. The whole Scripture, and particularly the whole Pauline Scripture, assures us what this does *not* mean. It does not mean the least suspension or distortion of the humanity or of the personality of Paul. It means no absorption of his *ego*, and nothing whatever *un*-natural in either the nature or the exercise of his affections. His "homesick longing" to see the dear Philippian people again is quite as simple, natural, personal, as any longing he ever felt in his boyhood for his home at Tarsus when he was absent from it. Yes, but this personality, working so freely and truly in its every faculty, is now, by the Holy Ghost, so put into spiritual contact with the will and heart of Jesus Christ, who now "dwells in it by faith," that the whole action moves, so to speak, in the sphere, in the atmosphere, of HIM. The love which passes so freely through and out of the believer to his brethren would not be what it is if the believer were not "in Christ." He is still all himself; nay, he is more than ever himself, being in the Lord; for indeed that blessed union has a genial and developing power upon its happy subject. But such is that power that it deeply qualifies the mental and spiritual action of the being who enters into it; never violates but always qualifies.

The fact, the experience, of course transcends our analysis. But it is not beyond our faith, nor beyond our reception and inward verification.

"Thy love, Thy joy, Thy peace,
 Continuously impart
 Unto my heart;
Fresh springs that never cease,
 But still increase." [7]

Our immediate purpose meanwhile is not to discuss the believer's union with his Lord, but to remark on this one precious result of it, the opening of his inmost sympathies to the sharers of the same blessing. We see that result displayed in all its brightness in this first paragraph of the Epistle; and we shall see it to the end. In the particular case of St Paul and the Philippians it was indeed a remarkable phenomenon. Here on the one side was a man who, not very many years before, had been the devotee of the Pharisaic creed, a creed which tended powerfully not to expand but to annihilate every sympathy which could touch "the Gentiles." Here on the other side were people whose life and thought had been moulded in the proud political and national ideas of a Roman *colonia*; no kindly atmosphere for the growth of affections which should be at once intense and comprehensive. But these two unlikely parties are now one, in the strongest and most beautiful union of thought and heart. If we may use again a word ventured just above, they are mutually (not confused but) fused together. Their whole beings have come into living touch, not on the surface merely but most of all in their depths. An interchange of idea, of sympathy, of purpose has become possible between them in which, while self-respect is only deepened and secured, reserve is melted away in the common possession of the life and love of Jesus Christ. The Apostle writes to his friends as one whose whole soul is open to them, is at their command. His memory and reflexion are full of them. He not only prays and gives thanks for them but delights in telling them that he is doing so. He says without difficulty exactly what he is sure of about them, and exactly what things he is asking for them as yet more developed blessings. Above all, the name of Him who is everything to himself and to them flows from his heart with a holy freedom which is impossible except where the parties in religious intercourse are indeed "one" in Him. Seven times in these eleven short verses "Christ Jesus" is explicitly named; as the writer's Possessor; as the Philippian saints' Life and Head; as the Giver to them, with His Father, of grace and peace; as the Lord of the longed-for "Day," that dear goal of hope; as the mighty Sphere of regenerate family-love; as the Cause and Condition of the Christian's fruitfulness for God. His presence, as it were, moves in the whole message, in the whole intercourse of which the message is the expression. Writer and readers perfectly "understand each other," for they both know Christ, and are found in Him.

The same divine Cause tends always to similar effects. Unhappily it does not always act without obstruction—obstruction which need not be. There are no doubt obstructions to its action which are inherent in our mortality; things which have to do really with physical temperament, or again with external circumstances which we may be helpless to modify. But the Cause, *in itself, tends always* to the effects visible in this noble passage of Christian affection. The possession and knowledge of Jesus Christ, in spirit and in truth, tends always, by an eternal law, to warm and open as well as to purify the human heart; to anchor it indeed immoveably to God, but also to suffuse it with a gracious sympathy towards man, and first and most of all towards man who is also, in Christ, cognizant of the "free-masonry" of faith.

Let this be our first main Lesson in Faith and Love in our Philippian studies. The section which we have traversed is full of points of interest and importance otherwise; but this aspect of it is so truly dominant that we may rightly take it for the true message of the whole. Let us welcome it home. Let us question ourselves, in presence of it, and before our Lord, first about our personal possession of the Cause, and then about our personal manifestation of the effects. Let us put to our own hearts some very old-fashioned interrogations: *Am I indeed in Jesus Christ? Is He to me indeed Possessor, Lord, Giver of grace and peace? Is my life so lived and my work so done in contact with Him that through Him, and not merely through myself, "my fruit is found"? Is His promised Day the goal and longing of my heart, as I submit myself to Him that He may perfect His work in me by the way, and watch over myself that I may meet Him single-hearted and "without offence" at the end? Is He the pervading and supreme Interest of my life? Is He the inward Power which colours my thought and gives direction and quality to my affections?*

No answer which a heart fully wakeful to God can give to such deliberate inward questionings can possibly be an easy or "light-hearted" answer. The gladdest and most thankful utterance of such a heart will carry along with it always the prayer, "Search me, O God, and try my heart"; "Enter not into judgment with Thy servant." Yet we are assuredly meant, if we are in Christ, so to know the fact as to rejoice in it, and to be strong in it; we are invited, without a doubt, so to know Him as to know we know Him, and to find in Him "all our salvation, and all our desire." Let us not rest till, in great humility but with perfect simplicity, we so see Him as to leave behind our doubts about our part and lot in Him, and, "believing, to rejoice."

And then let us covet the developement of those results of possession of Christ, of union with Christ, which we have specially studied in the opening section of our Epistle. Let us welcome the Lord in to "the springs of thought and will," with the conscious aim that He should so warm and enrich them with His presence that they shall overflow for blessing around us, in the life of Christian love. I do not mean for a moment that we should set ourselves to construct a spiritual mannerism of speech or of habit. The matter is one not of manufacture but of culture; it is a call to "nourish and cherish" the gift of God which is in us, and to give to it the humble co-operation of our definite wish and will that it may be *manifested* in the ways commended in His Word. It is a call to desire and intend to "*adorn* the doctrine of God our Saviour," in the outcoming of His presence in us in our tone, temper, and converse, towards those around us, and especially where we know that a common faith and common love do subsist.

If I mistake not, there is far too little of this at present, even in true Christian circles. A certain dread of "phraseology," of "pietism," of what is foolishly called "goody-goody," has long been abroad; a grievously exaggerated dread; a mere parody of rightful jealousy for sincerity in religion. Under the baneful spell of this dread it is only too common for really earnest Christians to keep each other's company, and even to take part in united religious work, and to be constantly together as worshippers, aye, perhaps as ministers of the Word and Ordinances of Christ, and yet never, or hardly ever, to exchange a word about HIM, heart to heart; still less to "speak often one to another," and share fully together their treasures of experience of what He is and what He has done for them. The very dialect of the Christian life has greatly lost in holy depth and tenderness, so it seems to me, since a former generation in which this over-drawn fear (it is a mere fashion) of "phraseology" was less prevalent. It ought not so to be.

Let us each for himself come closer to our eternal FRIEND, converse more fully with Him, "consider HIM" much more than many of us do. And then we too shall discover that "our mouth is opened, our heart enlarged," for holy converse with our fellow-servants, in that wonderful interchange of souls which is possible "in the heart of Jesus Christ."

"Oh days of heaven, and nights of equal praise,
Serene and peaceful as those heavenly days,
When souls, drawn upwards in communion sweet,
Enjoy the stillness of some close retreat;
Discourse, as if releas'd and safe at home,
Of dangers past and wonders yet to come,
And spread the sacred treasures of the breast
Upon the lap of covenanted rest." [8]

[1] *Sun episcopois kai diakonois.* I render the words as literally as possible, not to discredit the distinctive functions of the Christian ministry, but to remind the reader of the natural origin of the titles by which Christian ministers are designated. And it is important here to remember that our word *bishop*, while derived from *episkopos*, cannot properly translate it *as it is used in the New Testament*. For *episkopos* is not used there as the special title of a superintendent pastor set over other pastors. Such superintendents, however the office originated, are found in the New Testament, and early in the second century are called distinctively *episkopoi*: but the term so used is later, on any theory, than the origin of the office. But I do not purpose in these devotional chapters to discuss at length such a question as that raised here. The reader should by all means consult Bishop Lightfoot's Excursus in his Commentary on this Epistle, *The Christian Ministry*. The views advanced in that essay were, as I personally know, held by the writer to the last.

[2] The middle suggests a certain fulness of action.

[3] I think the definite article should be supplied in English; the reference is to the work of works.

[4] I give both the possible renderings of *huper*. Both would certainly be in place, as he thought of them and prayed and gave thanks for them.

[5] The derivation is doubtful, but the idea of the word in usage is clearness, freedom from complication.

[6] With some hesitation I assign to *dikaiosune* here the meaning of the righteousness of justification, as in iii. 9.

[7] F. R. Havergal.

[8] Cowper, *Conversation*.

# THE APOSTLE'S POSITION AND CIRCUMSTANCES

"Yield to the Lord, with simple heart,
All that thou hast and all thou art,
Renounce all strength but strength divine,
And peace shall be for ever thine."
    MME DE LA MOTHE GUYON, *translated by* COWPER.

# CHAPTER III

PHILIPPIANS i. 12-20

Disloyal "brethren"—Interest of the paragraph—The victory of patience—
The Praetorian sentinel—Separatism, and how it was met—St Paul's secret—
His "earnest expectation"—"Christ magnified"—"In my body"

St Paul has spoken his affectionate greeting to the Philippians, and has opened
to them the warm depths of his friendship with them in the Lord. What he
feels towards them "in the heart of Christ Jesus," what he prays for them in
regard of the growth and fruit of their new life, all has been expressed. It is
time now to meet their loving anxieties with some account of his own
position, and the circumstances of the mission in the City. Through this
passage let us follow him now; we shall find that the quiet picture, full of
strong human interest in its details, is suffused all over with the glory of the
presence and the peace of Christ.

Ver. 12. +Now I wish you to know, brethren, that my position and
circumstances+ (*ta kat eme*, "*the things related to me*") +have come out+,
have resulted, +rather for the progress of the Gospel+ message and enter-

Ver. 13. prise, than otherwise; +so that my bonds+, my imprisonment, with its
*custodia militaris*, +are become unmistakable+ (*phanerous*) as being +in
Christ+; as due to no social or political crime, but to the name and cause of
the Messiah of Israel, the Saviour of the world. This is the case in the +whole
Praetorium+,[1] in all ranks of the Imperial Guard, +and among other people
in general+ (*tois loipois pasi*[2]). And

Ver. 14. another result is[3] +that the majority+ (*tous plaionas*) +of the
brethren in the Lord+, the converts of the Roman mission, +feeling a new
confidence in connexion with my bonds+,[4] animated by the fact of my
imprisonment, realizing afresh the glory of the cause which makes me happy
to suffer, +venture more abundantly+, more frequently, more openly,
+fearlessly to speak the Word+, the message of Christ, of the Cross, of Truth,
of Life. There is a drawback in this

Ver. 15. welcome phenomenon: +some indeed actually+ (*kai*) +for envy and
strife, while others as truly+ (*kai*) +for goodwill, are proclaiming the Christ+.
The latter[5]

Ver. 16. are at work thus +from+ motives of love, love to the Lord and to me

His captive Messenger, +knowing+ that on purpose +for the vindication+ (*apologian*) +of the Gospel I am posted+ (*keimai*, as a soldier, fixed by his captain's order) here. The former from

Ver. 17. motives of +faction+, partizanship (*eritheia*) in a self-interested propaganda of their own opinions, +are announcing the Christ, not purely, thinking+ and meaning +to raise up+ (*egeirein*, so read) +tribulation for+ me in +my bonds+; as so easily they can do, by detaching from me many converts who would otherwise gather round me, and generally by the mortifying thought of their freedom and activity in contrast to my enforced isolation. Shall I give way to the trial, and lose patience and peace? Must I? Need

Ver. 18. I? Nay; +what matters it+ (*ti gar*)? Is not the fiery arrow quenched in Christ for me? Is it not thus nothing to me? Yes—yet not nothing, after all; for it brings a gain; it spreads the Gospel so much further; so that to my "What matters it?" I may add, +Only, in every way+, fair or foul, +Christ is being announced; and in this I rejoice, aye, and rejoice I shall+; the future can only bring me fresh reasons for a joy which lies wholly in the triumphs of my Lord, and can only bring fresh blessings to

Ver. 19. me His vassal. +For I know that I shall find+ (*moi*) this experience +result in salvation+, in the access of saving grace to my soul, +through your supplication+ for me, which will be quickened by your knowledge of my trials, +and+ through a resulting +full supply+ (*epichorêgia*: the word suggests a supply which is ample) +of the Spirit of Jesus Christ+; a developed presence in me of the Holy Ghost, coming from the exalted Saviour, and revealing Him, and applying Him. Such blessing will be exactly

Ver. 20. +according to my eager expectation+ (*apokaradokia*) and hope, that in no respect shall I be disappointed (*aiochunthêsomai*: with the "shame" of a miscalculation), +but that in all outspokenness+ (*parrêsia*) of testimony, whether in word or deed, +as always, so also now, Christ shall be magnified in my body, whether by means of life or by means of death+.

The passage is full of various points of interest. It is interesting, as we saw in our first chapter, in regard of the historical criticism of the Epistle. It gives a strong suggestion (I follow Lightfoot in the remark) in favour of dating the Epistle early in the "two years" of Acts xxviii. For it implies that the fact of the Apostle's imprisonment was a powerful stimulant to the zeal of the Roman Christians; and this is much more likely to have been the case when the imprisonment was still a new fact to them, than later. St Paul's arrival and first settlement, in the character (totally new in Rome, so far as we know) of a "prisoner of Jesus Christ," would of itself give a quickening shock, so to speak, to the believing community, which had suffered, so we gather, from a certain decadence of zeal. But when he had been some time amongst them, and the conditions of the "hired house" had become usual and familiar in their thoughts, it would be otherwise; whatever else about St Paul might rekindle their ardour, the mere fact of his imprisoned state would hardly do so.

The passage is further interesting as it indicates one particular direction of the Apostle's influence upon the pagans around him. It was felt, primarily, "in all the Praetorium," that is to say, in the large circle of the Imperial Life-guards. [6] We gather here, with reasonable certainty, that from the Life-guards were supplied, one by one, "the soldiers that kept him" (Acts xxviii. 16); mounting guard over him in turn, and fastened to him by the long chain which clasped at one end the wrist of the prisoner, at the other that of the sentinel. It needs only a passing effort of imagination to understand something of the exquisite trial to every sensibility which such a custody must have involved, even where the conditions were favourable. Let the guardian be ever so considerate and civil, it would be a terrible ordeal to be literally never alone, night or day; and too often, doubtless, the guardian would be not at all complaisant. To many a man, certainly to any man of the refined mental and moral nature of St Paul, this slow fire of indescribable annoyance would be far worse to endure than a great and sudden infliction of pain, even to death. It is a noble triumph of grace when such a test is well borne, and turned by patience into an occasion for God. When Nicholas Ridley, for a long year and a half (1554-5) was committed at Oxford to the vexatious domestic custody of the mayor and his bigoted wife, Edmund and Margaret Irish, it must have been nothing less than a slow torture to one whose fine nature had been used for years to the conditions of civil and ecclesiastical dignity and of a large circle of admirable friends. And it was a spiritual victory, second only to that of his glorious martyrdom (Oct. 16, 1555), when the close of that dreary time found the once obdurate and vexatious Mrs Irish won by Ridley's life to admiration and attachment, and also, as it would seem, to scriptural convictions.[7] But it was a still nobler result from a still more persistent and penetrating trial when St Paul so lived and so witnessed in the presence of this succession of Roman soldiers that the whole Guard was pervaded with a knowledge of his true character and position, evidently in the sense of interest and of respect. It must have been a course of *unbroken* consistency of conduct as well as of openness of witness. Had he only sometimes, only rarely, only once or twice, failed in patience, in kindness, in the quiet dignity of the Gospel, the whole succession of his keepers would have felt the effect, as the story passed from one to another. As a fact, the "keeping power of Christ" was always with him, and always used by him, and the men went out one after another to say that here was a prisoner such as never was before. Here was no conspirator or criminal; his "bonds" were evidently (ver. 13) due only to his devotion to a

God whom he would not renounce, and whose presence with him and power over him were visibly shewn in the divine peace and love of his hourly life.

We can please ourselves if we will by imagining many a scene for the exercise of that influence. Sometimes the Saint would be left much alone with the Praetorian. Sometimes a long stream of visitors would flow in, and for a whole day perhaps the two would scarcely exchange a word; the Guardsman would only watch and listen, if he cared to do so. Sometimes it would be a case where ignorant and ribald blasphemies would have to be met in the power of the peace of God. Sometimes a really wistful heart would at once betray its presence under the Roman cuirass. Perhaps the man would attack the Apostle with ridicule, or with enquiries, after some long day of religious debate, such as that recorded in Acts xxviii., and the silent night would see St Paul labouring on to win this soul also.

> "These ears were dull to Grecian speech;
>   This heart more dull to aught but sin;
> Yet the great Spirit bade thee reach,
>   Wake, change, exalt, the soul within:
> I've heard; I know; thy Lord, ev'n He,
> JESUS, hath look'd from heaven on me.

\* \* \* \* \*

> "A Christian, yes—for ever now
> A Christian: so our Leader keep
> My faltering heart: to Him I bow,
> His, whether now I wake or sleep:
> In peace, in battle. His:—the day
> Breaks in the east: oh, once more pray!" [8]

The passage before us is interesting again because of the light it throws on the very early rise of a separatist movement in the Roman mission-church, and on the principles on which St Paul met it. Extremely painful and perplexing the phenomenon was, though by no means new in its nature to St Paul, as we well know. It was a trouble altogether from within, not from without. The men who "preached Christ of envy and strife" bore evidently the Christian name as openly as their sincerer brethren. They were baptized members of the community of the Gospel. And their evangelization was such that St Paul was able to say, "Christ is preached"; though this does not mean, assuredly, that there were no doubtful elements mingled in the preaching. Now for them, as for all the Roman Christians, he had every reason to regard himself as the Lord's appointed centre of labour and of order. There he was, the divinely commissioned Apostle of Christ, at once the Teacher and the Leader of the Gentile Churches; only a few short years before he had written to these very people, in his inspired and commissioned character, the greatest of the Epistles. Yet now behold a separation, a schism. That such the movement was we cannot doubt. These "brethren," he tells us, carried on their missionary efforts in a way precisely intended to "raise up trouble" for him in his prison. The least that they would do with that object would be not only to teach much that he would disapprove of, but to intercept intercourse between their converts and him; to ignore him altogether as the central representative of the Church at Rome; to arrange for assemblies, to administer Baptisms, to practise the Breaking of Bread, wholly apart from the order and cohesion which he would sanction, and which he had the fullest right to enjoin. All this was a great evil, a sin, carrying consequences which might affect the Christian cause far and wide. Is it not true that no deliberate schism has ever taken place in the Church where there has not been grievous sin in the matter—on one side, or, on the other, or on both?

Yet how does the Apostle meet this distressing problem? With all the large tolerance and self-forgetting patience which come to the wise man who walks close to God in Christ. No great leader, surely, ever prized more the benefits of order and cohesion than did St Paul. And where a fundamental error was in view, as for example that about Justification in Galatia, no one could meet it more energetically, and with a stronger sense of authority, than he did. But he "discerned things that differ." And when, as here, he saw around him men, however misguided, who were aiding in the "announcement" of the Name and salvation of Christ, he thought more of the evangelization than of the breach of coherence, which yet most surely he deplored. He speaks with perfect candour of the unsound spiritual state of the separatists, their envy, strife, and partizanship. But he has no anathema for their methods. He is apparently quite unconscious of the thought that because he is the one Apostle in Rome grace can be conveyed only through him; that his authority and commission are necessary to authenticate teaching and to make ordinances effectual. He would far rather have order, and he knows that he is its lawful centre. But "the announcement of Christ" is a thing even more momentous than order. He cannot stay to speak of that great but inferior benefit, while he "rejoices, aye, and is going to rejoice," in the diffusion of the Name and salvation of the Lord.

It is an instructive lesson. Would that in all the after ages the Church had more watchfully followed this noble precedent! The result would have been, so I venture to hold, a far truer and stronger cohesion, in the long run, than we see, alas, around us now.

What was the secret of this happy harmony of the love of order and the capacity for tolerance in the mind of St Paul? It was a secret as deep but also as simple as possible; it was the Lord Jesus Christ. Really and literally, Jesus Christ was the one ruling consideration for St Paul; not himself, his claims, position, influence, feelings; not even the Church. To him the Church was inestimably precious, but the Lord was more. And all his thoughts about work, authority, order, and the like, were accordingly conditioned and governed by the thought, What will best promote the glory of the Lord who loved us and gave Himself for us? If even a separatist propaganda will extend the knowledge of HIM, His servant can rejoice, not in the separatism, not in the unhappy spirit which prompted it, but in the extension of the reign of Jesus Christ in the human hearts which need Him. Surely, even in our own day, with its immemorial complications of the question of exterior order, it will tend more than anything else to straighten the crooked places and level the rough places, if we look, from every side, on the glory of the blessed Name as our supreme and ruling interest.

This view of the supremacy of the Saviour in the thoughts of St Paul about the Church leads us to a view, as we close, of that supremacy in all his thoughts about his own life. Our paragraph ends with the words which anticipate a great blessing, a new developement of "salvation," in the writer's soul, in answer to the believing prayers of the Philippians; and then comes the thought that this result will carry out his dearest personal ambition—"that Christ may be magnified in my body, whether by life or by death." Let us take up those final words for a simple study, before God.

"According to my eager expectation," my *apokaradokia*, my waiting and watching, with outstretched head, for some keenly wished-for arrival, or attainment. Such is this man's thought and feeling with regard to the "magnification" of Christ through his life and death. It is his "hope," it is his absorbing "expectation." It is to him the thing with which he wakes up in the morning, and over which he lingers as he prepares to sleep at night. It is the animating inner interest which gives its zest to life. What art is to the ambitious and successful painter, what literature is to the man who loves it for its own sake and whose books have begun to take the world, what athletic toil and triumph is to the youth in his splendid prime, what the fact of extending and wealth-winning enterprise is to the man conscious of mercantile capacity —all this, only very much more, is the "magnification of Christ in his body" to the prisoner who sits, never alone, in the Roman lodging. It is this which effectually forbids him ever to find the days dull. Its light falls upon everything; comforts, trials, days of toil, hours of comparative repose, prospects of life, prospects of death. It quickens and concentrates all his faculties, as a great and animating interest always tends to do; it is always present to his mind as light and heat, to his will as rest and power. It secures for him the quiet of a great disengagement and liberty from selfish motives; it continually drives him on, with a force which does not exhaust him (for it is from above) in the ambition and enterprise which is for Christ; giving him at once an impulse toward great and arduous labours, and a patience and loving tact which continually adjusts itself to the smallest occasions of love and service.

Reader, this is admirable in St Paul. But after all, the ultimate secret of the noble phenomenon resides not in St Paul but in Jesus Christ. "It pleased God to reveal His Son in me" (Gal. i. 15, 16). The man had seen his Saviour with his whole soul. And because of—not the man who saw but—the Saviour who was seen, behold, the life is lifted off the pivot of self-will and transferred to that of "the glory of God in the face of Jesus Christ." The same "revealing" grace can lift us also. We are not St Pauls; but the Jesus Christ of St Paul is absolutely the same, in Himself, for us. We will, in His name, place ourselves in the way of His working, that He may so shew us His fair countenance that we may *not be able not* to live, quite really, for Him as the enthralling Interest of life.

Let us look at the words again: "That Christ may be *magnified*," may be made great. In what respect? Not in Himself; for He is already "all in all"; "filling all things"; "higher than the heavens." Such is He that "no man knoweth the Son but the Father"; the mind of Deity is alone adequate to comprehend His glory. But He may be magnified—relatively to those who see Him, or may see Him. To eyes which find in Christ only a distant and obscure Object, however sacred, He may be made to occupy the whole field of the soul with His love and glory. As when the telescope is directed upon the heavens, and some "cloudy spot" becomes, magnified, a mighty planet perhaps, or perhaps a universe of starry suns; so it is when through a believer's life "Christ is magnified" to eyes which watch that life and see the reality of the power within.

Ah, have we not known such lives ourselves? Has not the Lord been made very near to us, and very luminous, in the face of father, mother, brother, sister, friend, or pastor? Have we not seen Him shining large and near us in their holy activities, and in their blessed sufferings, shedding His glory through all they were and all they did? He has been magnified to us by saints in high places, whose dignity and fame have been to them only so much occasion for the exercise of their "ruling passion"—the glory of Christ. And He has been magnified to us also by saints in comfortless cottages, imprisoned upon sick-beds in gloomy attics, but finding in everything an occasion to experience and to manifest the power of their Lord. May He make it always our ambition to be thus His magnifiers. But may He keep it a really pure ambition. For even this can be distorted into the misery of self-seeking;

an ambition not that Christ may be magnified, but that His magnifier may be thought "some great one" in the spiritual life.

"In my *body*." Because through the body, and only through it, practically, can we tell on others for the Lord. Do we speak to them? Do we write to them? Do we make home comfortable and happy for them? Do we "meet the glad with joyful smiles and wipe the weeping eyes"? Do we travel to those who want us? Do we nurse them? Do we think for them? All has its motives in the regenerate spirit, but all has its effect through the body. Without brain, eyes, ears, lips, hands, feet—how could we serve, how could we shine? Our life would have no articulation to others, nor our death.

"I beseech you therefore, brethren, by the mercies of God, that ye present *your bodies* a living sacrifice." So be it, for writer and for reader. Then blessed will be our life, as day by day brings ceaseless occasions for the pursuit of our dear ambition—"that Christ may be magnified."

———

\*\*\* *En holô tô praitôriô* (ver. 13).—The word *praitôrion* occurs in e.g. Matt. xxvii. 27. Acts xxiii. 35, in the sense of the residence of a great official, regarded as *praetor*, or commander. The A.V. here evidently reasons from such passages, and takes the word to mean the residence at Rome of the supreme *praetor*, the Emperor; the *Palatium*, the vast range of buildings on the Mons Palatinus which has since given a name to all "palaces." Bishop Lightfoot however has made it clear (*a*) that such a use at Rome, by Romans, of the word *Praetorium* was probably not known; (*b*) that the word *Praetorium* was a familiar word for the great body of the Imperial Life-guards; and that it would probably be often so used by the (praetorian) "soldiers who kept him." On the whole it seems clear that, at Rome, the word would denote a body, not a place. It never appears as a name for the great *camp* of the Praetorians, outside Rome at the east.

[1] See note at the end of this chapter.

[2] The A.V. rendering "in all other *places*" is obviously due to the belief that *praitôrion* signified a place, not a body of men.

[3] I thus convey the force of *hoste*, across the break we have made in the original sentence.

[4] Literally perhaps, "relying on my bonds," as a new *ground* for their assurance of the goodness of the cause.—It is possible to render here, "the brethren, *having in the Lord confidence*, are, in view of my bonds, much more bold," etc. But the rhythm of the Greek is in favour of our rendering (which is essentially that of A.V. and R.V.).

[5] I adopt here the order of the Greek clauses which is best attested.

[6] See note at the end of this chapter.

*[7]* I venture to refer to my book, *Bishop Ridley on the Lord's Supper* (Seeley), pp. 54, 55, 72.

[8] See the close of the volume.

# THE CHRISTIAN'S PEACE AND THE CHRISTIAN'S CONSISTENCY

O God, from whom all holy desires, all good counsels, and all just works do proceed; Give unto Thy servants that peace which the world cannot give; that both our hearts may be set to obey Thy commandments, and also that by Thee we being defended from the fear of our enemies may pass our time in rest and quietness; through the merits of Jesus Christ our Saviour. Amen.

*The Second Collect at Evening Prayer.*

# CHAPTER IV

## THE CHRISTIAN'S PEACE AND THE CHRISTIAN'S CONSISTENCY

PHILIPPIANS i. 21-30

He will be spared to them—Spiritual wealth of the paragraph—Adolphe
Monod's exposition—Charles Simeon's testimony—The equilibrium and its
secret—The intermediate bliss—He longs for their full consistency—The
"gift" of suffering

Ver. 21. +For to me, to live is Christ+; the consciousness and experiences of
living, in the body, are so full of Christ, my supreme Interest, that CHRIST
sums them all up; +and to die+, the act of dying,[1] +is gain+, for it will usher
me in from an existence of blessing to an existence of more blessing still.
+But+

Ver. 22. +if living+ on, +in the flesh+, be my lot; if the present suspense
issues in my being acquitted at the Roman tribunal, +this will prove to me+
(*touto moi*) +fruit of work+; it will just mean so much more work for the
Lord, and so much more fruit; I shall welcome it not as being the best thing in
itself, as if I chose mortal life for its own sake, but because of its ceaseless
opportunities for my Lord. +And which+ alternative +I shall choose, I do not
know+, I do not *recognize* (*gnôrizô*, as one who seeks to be sure of the face of

Ver. 23. a friend amidst other faces). +Nay+ (*de*), +I am held in suspense on
both sides+;[2] +my+ personal +desire being[3] in the direction of
departing+, striking my tent, weighing my anchor (*analysai*),[4] +and being
with Christ+ (for this is what "departing" means for us Christians, on its other
side); +for it is far, far better+, by far more preferable, *pollô mallon kreisson*
—aye even than a "life in the flesh" which "is Christ"! +But+

Ver. 24. then +the abiding by+ (*epimenein*) +the flesh+, the brave, faithful,
holding fast to the conditions of earthly trial, +is more necessary+, more
obligatory, more of the nature of duty as against pleasure, +on account of
you+, and your further need of me in the Lord. And +feeling+

Ver. 25. +confident of this, I know that I shall remain+—aye +and shall
remain side by side+ (*paramenô*) +with you all+, as your comrade, your
helper, +in order to your progress and joy in your faith+;[5] so as to promote
your growth in the exercise of loyal reliance on your Lord, and in the deep joy
which is the natural issue of such

Ver. 26. reliance; +so that your exultation may be overflowing in Christ

Jesus+, in your living union with Him, +in me+ (*en emoi*), "in" whom you see a living example of your Lord's love, shewn to you +by means of my+

Ver. 27. +coming back to you again+. +Only+, whether I am thus actually restored to you or not, +order your life[6] in a way worthy of the Gospel of Christ+ (above all, worthy of the unifying, harmonizing power of the Gospel); +so that whether coming and seeing you, or+ remaining +absent, I may hear[7] about your circumstances+, your condition, +that you are standing firm in One Spirit+,[8] in the power of the One Strengthener, and, +with one soul+, one life and love, the resultant of the One Spirit's work in you all, +wrestling side by side+, with enemies and obstacles, +for [9]the faith of the Gospel+, for the maintenance and victory of that reliance which embraces

Ver. 28. the truth of Christ; +and refusing to be+ (*mê*) +scared out of that attitude in anything by your+ (*tôn*) +opponents+, the unconverted world around you. +Such+ (*hêtis*) calm united courage +is to them an evidence+, a sure token, an omen, +of+ the +perdition+ which awaits the obstinate foes of holiness, +but to you of+ the +salvation+ which awaits Christ's faithful witnesses. +And this, this+ condition of conflict and courage, +is from God+; no mere blind result of accidents, but His purpose.

Ver. 29. Yes, +because to you there has been granted[10] as an+ actual +boon —for the sake of Christ not only the believing on Him but also the suffering for His sake+;[11] a sacred privilege when it is involved by

Ver. 30. loyalty to such a Master! So you will be +experiencing+[12] (*echontes*) +the same conflict in kind+ (*oion*) (as you wrestle side by side for your Lord against evil) +as that which you saw in me+, in my case, when I was with you in those first days (Acts xvi.), *and* which *you now hear of in me*, as I meet it in my prison at Rome.

The translation of our present section is completed. It has presented rather more material than usual for grammatical remark and explanation; constructions have proved to be complex, contracted, or otherwise slightly anomalous; and points of order and emphasis have claimed attention. But I trust that this handling of *the texture* has only brought more vividly into sight the holy richness and brightness of *the design*. Sentence by sentence, we have been reading a message of the first order of spiritual importance, as St Paul has spoken from his own experience of the Christian's wonderful happiness in life and death, and then, in his appeal to the Philippians, of the Christian's path of love and duty.

Let us listen anew to each part of that precious message.

i. The Christian's Happiness in Life and Death.

In Adolphe Monod's volume of death-bed addresses, his *Adieux à ses Amis et à l'Eglise*, one admirable chapter, the second, is devoted to the passage before us, Phil. i. 21-26. From the borderland of eternity the great French Christian looks backward and forward with St Paul's letter in his hand, and comments there upon this divine possibility of "Happiness in Life and in Death." "The Apostle," he says, "is asking here which is most worth while for him, to live or to die. Often has that question presented itself to us, and perhaps we, like the Apostle, have answered that 'we are in a strait.' But I fear we may have used the words in a sense far different from St Paul's. When we have wished for death, we meant to say, 'I know not which alternative I ought most to dread, the afflictions of life, from which death would release me, or the terrors of death, from which life protects me.' In other words, life and death look to us like two evils of which we know not which is the less. As for the Apostle, they look to him like two immense blessings, of which he knows not which is the better. Personally, he prefers death, in order to be with Christ. As regards the Church and the world, he prefers life, in order to serve Jesus Christ, to extend His kingdom, and to win souls for Him. What an admirable view of life and of death!—admirable, because it is all governed (*dominiée*), all sanctified, by love, and is akin to the Lord Jesus Christ's own view of life and death. Let us set ourselves to enter into this feeling (*sentiment*). Life is good; death is good. Death is good, because it releases us from the miseries of this life, but above all because, even were life full for us of all the joys which earth can give, death bids us enter into a joy and a glory of which we can form no idea. We are then to consider death as a thing desirable in itself. Let us not shun what serves to remind us of it. Let all the illnesses, all the sudden deaths, all that passes round us, remind us that for each one of us death may come at any moment. But then life also is good, because in life we can serve, glorify, imitate, Jesus Christ. Life is not worth the trouble of living for any other object. All the strength we possess, all the breath, the life, the faculties, all is to be consecrated, devoted, sanctified, crucified, for the service of our Lord Jesus Christ. This crucified life is the happy life, even amidst earth's bitterest pains; it is the life in which we can both taste for ourselves and diffuse around us the most precious blessings. Let us love life, let us feel the value of life—but to fill it with Jesus Christ. In order to such a state of feeling, the Holy Spirit alone can transform us into new men. But observe; it is not only that *our spirit* must be sustained, consoled, fortified; *the Spirit of God* must come to dwell in us. We often set ourselves to work on ourselves, to set our spirit in order; this is well, but it is not enough. We want more. Jesus Christ Himself must dwell in our hearts by the Holy Spirit.

"My friends, let us reflect upon the character of the promises of the Gospel, and we shall see how far we are from possessing and enjoying them. May

God open the heavens above our heads; revealing all to us, filling us with all wisdom, granting us to see that even here below we may attain to perfect joy, while looking forward to possess hereafter the plenitude of bliss and of victory. May He teach us how to gather up the blessings which the heavens love to pour upon the earth which opens to receive them. And so may He teach us to know that if earth is able to bear us down and trouble us, it is unable to quench the virtues of heaven, to annul the promises of God, or to throw a veil, be it even the lightest cloud, over the love with which God has loved us in Jesus Christ."[13]

"He being dead yet speaketh." On his bed of prolonged and inexpressible sufferings Monod, called comparatively early to leave a life and ministry of singular fruitfulness and rich in interests, found in Jesus the inexhaustible secret of this blessed *equilibrium* of St Paul. And what a cloud of witnesses have borne their testimony to that same open secret, as the most solid while most supernatural of realities! As I write, the memory comes up before me of a beloved friend and kinsman, my contemporary at Cambridge, called unexpectedly to die in his twenty-second year. Life to him was full of the strongest interests and most attractive hopes, alike in nature and in grace. He had no quarrel with life; it had poured out before him a rich store of social and mental blessings, and a large wealth of surrounding love, and the Lord Jesus, taking early and decisive possession of the young man's heart, had only augmented and glorified, not rebuked or stunted, every interest. But a slight fever, caught in the Swiss hotel, was medically mismanaged, and when perfect skill was summoned in, it was too late. His mother came to her son on his sofa to tell him that he was not only, as he knew, very poorly; he was about to die. In a moment, without a change of colour, without a tremor, without a pause, smiling a radiant smile, he looked up and answered, "Well, to depart and to be with Christ is far better!"

So the young Christian passed away, exchanging life which was sweet for death which, because of the life it would reveal, was sweeter. And "the veterans of the King" say just the same. If ever a man enjoyed life, with a vigorous and conscious joy, it was Simeon of Cambridge. And till the age of exactly seventy-seven he was permitted to *live* with a powerful life indeed; a life full of affections, interests, enterprises, achievements, and all full of Christ. Yet in that energetic and intensely human soul "the *desire* was to depart and to be with Christ." It was no dreamy reverie; but it was supernatural. It stimulated him to unwearied work; but it was breathed into him from eternity. "I cannot but run with all my might," he wrote in the midst of his youthful old age, *"for I am close to the goal."*

It is indeed a phenomenon peculiar to the Gospel, this view of life and death.

It is far more than resignation. It is different even from the "holy indifference" of the mystic saints. For it is full of warmth, and sympathy, and all the affections of the heart, *in both directions*. The man who is the happy possessor of this secret does not on the one hand go about saying to himself that all around him is *maya*, is a dream, a phantasm of the desert sands counterfeiting the waters and the woods of Eden. He is as much alive in human life as the worldling is, and more. He cordially loves his dear ones; he is the open-hearted friend, the helpful neighbour, the loving and loyal citizen and subject, the attentive and intelligent worker in his daily path of duty. Time with its contents is full of reality and value to him. He does not hold that the earth is God-forsaken. With his Lord (Ps. civ.), he "rejoices in the works" of that Lord's hands; and, with the heavenly Wisdom (Prov. viii.), "his delights are with the sons of men." But on the other hand, he does not banish from his thoughts as if it were unpractical the dear prospect of another world. He is not foolish enough to talk of "other-worldliness," as if it were a selfish thing to "lay up treasure in heaven," and so to have "his heart there also." For him the present could not possibly be what it is in its interests, affections, and purposes, if it were not for the revealed certainties of an everlasting future in the presence of the King. "He faints not," in the path of genuine temporal toil and duty, because "he looks at the things which are not seen."

But now, what is the secret of the equilibrium? We saw in our last chapter what was the secret of the unruffled peace with which St Paul could meet the exquisite trials occasioned by the separatist party at Rome. It was the Lord Jesus Christ. And the secret of the far more than peace with which here he meets the alternative of life and death is precisely the same; it is the Lord Jesus Christ. He has no philosophy of happiness; he has something infinitely better; he has the Lord. What gives life its zest and charm for him? It is, that life "is Christ." What makes death an object of positive personal "desire" for him, matched, let us remember, against a "life" with which he is so deeply contented? It is, that "to depart" is to be with Christ, which is "far, far better." On either side of the veil, Jesus Christ is all things to him. So both sides are divinely good; only, the conditions of the other side are such that the longed-for companionship of his MASTER will be more perfectly realized there.

We might linger long over this golden passage. It would give us matter for more than one chapter to unfold adequately, for example, its clear witness to the conscious and immediate blessedness in death of the servants of God. We may ponder long what it implies in this direction when we remember that its "far, far better" means "better" not than our present life at its worst but than our present life at its holiest and best; for, as we have observed already, it is "far, far better" than a life here which "is Christ." Whatever mysteries attend the thought of the Intermediate State, and however distinctly we remember that the *disembodied* spirit must, as such, be circumstanced less perfectly than the spirit lodged again in the body, "the body of glory," yet this at least we gather here; the believer's happy spirit, "departing" from "this tabernacle," finds itself not in the void, not in the dark, not under penal or disciplinary pain, but in a state "far, far better" than its very best yet. It is, in a sense so much better in degree as to be new in kind, "with Christ."

"Yes, think of all things at the best; in one rich thought unite
All purest joys of sense and soul, all present love and light;
Yet bind this truth upon thy brow and clasp it to thy heart,
And then nor grief nor gladness here shall claim too great a part—
All radiance of this lower sky is to that glory dim;
Far better to depart it is, for we shall be WITH HIM." [14]

ii. But even on this theme I must not linger now. Not only because "the time would fail me," but because we have to remember that *the main* incidence of the Apostle's thought here is not upon the blessedness of death but upon the joy of duty, the "fruit of labour," in continued life. He looks in through the gate, not to sigh because he may not enter yet, but "to run with all his might," in the path of unselfish service, "because he is close to the goal"—the goal of being with Christ, to whom he will belong for ever, and whom he will serve for ever, "day and night in His temple." He "knows that he shall remain, and that, side by side with" his dear converts at Philippi. And his "meat is to do the will of Him that sent him, and *to finish* His work."

The remainder of our chosen portion is altogether to this purpose. He has said enough about himself now, having just indicated how much Christ can be to him for peace and power in the great alternative. Now his thoughts are wholly at Philippi, and he spends himself on entreating them to live indeed, to live wholly for Christ; and to do so in two main respects, in self-forgetting unity, and in the recognition of the joy and glory of suffering.

"Only let them order their life in a way worthy of the Gospel of Christ." "*Only*"; as if this were the one possible topic for him now. This will content him; nothing else will. He "desires one thing of the Lord"—the practical holiness of his beloved converts; and he cannot possibly do otherwise, coming as he has just come from "the secret of the presence," felt in his own experience. Will they be watchful and prayerful? Will they renounce the life of self-will, and entirely live for their Lord's holy credit and glory? Will they particularly surrender a certain temptation to jealousies and divisions? Will they recollect that Christ has so committed Himself to them to manifest to the world that it is the "only" thing in life, after all, in the last resort, to be *practically* true to Him? Then the Missionary will be happy; his "joy will be fulfilled."

What pastor, what evangelist, what worker of any true sort for God in the souls of others, does not know something of the meaning of that "only" of the Apostle's?

Then he passes, by a transition easy indeed in the case of the Philippian saints, to the subject of suffering. In that difficult scene, the Roman *colonia*, to be perfectly consistent, must mean, in one measure or another, to suffer; it must mean to encounter "adversaries," such open adversaries, probably, as those who had dragged Paul and Silas to the judgment seat and the dungeon, ten years before. How were they to meet that experience, or anything resembling it? Not merely with resignation, nor even with resolution, but with a recognition of the joy, nay of the "*gift*," of "suffering for His sake."

Circumstances infinitely vary, and so therefore do sufferings. The Master assigns their kinds and degrees, not arbitrarily indeed but sovereignly; and it is His manifest will that not all equally faithful Christians should equally encounter open violence, or even open shame, "for His sake." But it is His will also, definitely revealed, that suffering in some sort, "for His name's sake," should normally enter into the lot of "all that will live godly in Christ Jesus." Even in the Church there is the world. And the world does not like the allegiance to Christ which quite refuses, however modestly and meekly, to worship its golden image. To the end, pain must be met with in the doing here on earth of the "beloved will of God."

But this very pain is "a gift" from the treasures of heaven. Not in itself; pain is never in itself a good; the perfect bliss will not include it; "there shall be no more pain." But in its relations and its effects it is "a gift" indeed. For to the disciple who meets it in the path of witness and of service for his Master amongst his fellows, it opens up, as nothing else can do, the fellowship of the faithful, and the heart of JESUS.

[1] Observe the aorist infinitive, *to apothanein*, of *the crisis*, dying, contrasted with the present infinitive, *to zên*, of *the process, living.*—It may be noticed that the renderings of Luther, *Christus ist mein Leben*, and Tindale, *Christ is to me lyfe*, are untenable, though expressing as a fact a deep and precious truth. The Apostle is obviously dealing with the characteristics, not the source, of "living."

[2] *Sunechomai*: literally, "I am confined, restricted from the two (sides)"; as if to say, "I am hindered as to my choice, whichever side you view me from."

[3] Literally, "having the desire"; not "a desire," which misses the point of the words. He means that his *epithymia* lies in one direction, his conviction of call and duty in the other. *The* desire, the element of personal longing in him, is for "departing."

37

[4] The Vulgate renders here, *cupio dissolvi*, as if *analysai* meant, so to speak, to "analyse" myself into my elements, to separate my soul from my body. But the usage of the verb, in the Greek of the Apocrypha, is for the sense given in our Versions, and above; to "break up," in the sense of "setting out."

[5] Literally, "your progress and joy of the faith." The Greek suggests the connexion of both "progress" and "joy" with "faith." And St Paul's general use of the word *pistis* favours its reference here not to the objective *creed* but to the subjective *reliance* of the holder of the creed.

[6] *Politeuesthe*: literally, "live your citizen-life." But in its usage the verb drops all *explicit* reference to the *politês*, and means little more than "live"; in the sense however not of mere existence, or even of experience, but of a course of principle and order. See Acts xxiii. 1, the only other N.T. passage where it occurs; and 2 Macc. vi. 1, xi. 25.

[7] The words suggest to us that the Apostle might have written, more fully and exactly, *hina idô, ean elthô, kai hina akousô, ean apô*. But it is best to retain in translation the somewhat lax grammatical form of the Greek.

[8] The parallels, 1 Cor. xii. 13, Eph. ii. 18, strongly favour the reference of *pneuma* here to the Holy Spirit of God.

[9] It is of course possible to translate *synathlountes tê piotei*, "wrestling side by side with the faith," as if "the faith" was the Comrade of the believers. But the context is not favourable to this; the emphasis seems to lie throughout on the believers' fellowship *with one another*.

[10] *Echaristhê*: the English perfect best represents here the Greek aorist.

[11] The Greek may be explained as if the Apostle had meant to write, *echaristhn to uper Christou paschein*, and then freely inserted the antecedent fact of *to pioieuein*.

[12] *Echontes*: the nominative participle takes us back grammatically to the construction previous to the sentences beginning *hêtis eotin k.t.a.*; which sentences may be treated as a parenthesis. I have attempted to convey this in a paraphrase.

[13] *Adieux*, ed. 1857, pp. 10-12.

[14] From the writer's volume of verse, *In the House of the Pilgrimage*.

"Lord, we expect to suffer here,
  Nor would we dare repine;
But give us still to find Thee near,
  And own us still for Thine.

"Let us enjoy, and highly prize,

These tokens of Thy love,
Till Thou shalt bid our spirits rise
To worship Thee above."
    NEWTON.

# UNITY IN SELF-FORGETFULNESS: THE EXAMPLE OF THE LORD

"Our glorious Leader claims our praise
For His own pattern giv'n;
While the long cloud of witnesses
Shew the same path to heav'n."
WATTS.

## CHAPTER V

UNITY IN SELF-FORGETFULNESS: THE EXAMPLE OF THE LORD

PHILIPPIANS ii. 1-11

Dissensions incident to activity—Arguments for heart-union—"No plunderer's prize"—"The name"—The tone of the great passage—What the "Kenôsis" cannot be—It guarantees the infallibility—Doctrine and life —"Only thou"

In the section which we studied last we found the Apostle coming to the weak point of the Christian life of the Philippians. On the whole, he was full of thankful and happy thoughts about them. Theirs was no lukewarm religion; it abounded in practical benevolence, animated by love to Christ, and it was evidently ready for joyful witness to the Lord, in face of opposition and even of persecution. But there was a tendency towards dissension and internal separation in the Mission Church; a tendency which all through the Epistle betrays its presence by the stress which the Apostle everywhere lays upon holy unity, the unity of love, the unity whose secret lies in the individual's forgetfulness of self.

Such dangers are always present in the Christian Church, for everywhere and always saints are still sinners. And it is a sad but undeniable fact of Christian history that the spirit of difference, dissension, antagonism, within the ranks of the believing, is not least likely to be operative where there is a generally diffused life and vigour in the community. A state of spiritual chill or lukewarmness may even favour a certain exterior tranquillity; for where the energies of conviction are absent there will be little energy for discussion and resistance in matters not merely secular. But where Christian life and thought, and the expression of it, are in power, there, unless the Church is particularly watchful, the enemy has his occasion to put in the seeds of the tares amidst the golden grain. The Gospel itself has animated the disciples' affections, and also their intellects; and if the Gospel is not diligently used as guide as well as stimulus, there will assuredly be collisions.

Almost every great crisis of life and blessing in the Church has shewn examples of this. It was thus in the period of the Reformation, the moment the law of love was forgotten by the powerful minds which were so wonderfully energized as well as liberated by the rediscovery of eternal truths long forgotten. It was thus again in the course of the Evangelical Revival in the last century, when holy men, whose whole natures had been warmed and vivified by a new insight for themselves into the fulness of Christ, were betrayed into discussions on the mysteries of grace carried on in the spirit rather of self than of love. "We that are in this tabernacle do groan, being burthened." The words are true of the believing individual; they are true also of the believing Church. That which is perfect is not yet come. In the inscrutable but holy progress of the plan of God in redemption towards its radiant goal, it is permitted that temptation should connect itself with our very blessings, both in the person and in the community. And our one antidote is to watch and pray, looking unto Jesus, and looking away from ourselves.

It was thus in measure at Philippi. And St Paul cannot rest about it. He plies them with every loving argument for the unity of love, ranging from the plea of attachment to himself up to the supreme plea of "the mind that was in Christ Jesus" when He came down from heaven. He has begun to address them thus already. And in the wonderful passage now before us he is to develope his appeal to the utmost, in the Lord's name.

Ver. 1. +If therefore+, in connexion with this theme of holy oneness of love and life, +there is such a thing as comfort+, encouragement (*paraklêsis*), +in Christ+, drawn from our common union with the Lord, if +there is such a thing as love's consolation+, the tender cheer which love can give to a beloved one by meeting his inmost wish, +if there is such a thing as Spirit-sharing+,[1] +if there are such things as hearts+ (*splagchna, viscera*) +and compassions+, feelings of human tenderness and attachment, through which I may appeal to you simply as a friend, and a friend in trouble,

Ver. 2. calling for your pity; +make full my joy+, drop this last ingredient into the cup of my thankful happiness for you, and bring the wine to the brim, +by being[2] of the same mind+ (*phronma*, feeling, attitude of mind), +feeling+ (*echontes*) +the same love+, "the same" on all sides, soul and soul together (*sympsychoi*) +in a+

Ver. 3. +mind which is unity itself+.[3] +Nothing+ (*muden*, implying of course prohibition) +in the way of+ (*kata*) +personal or party spirit;[4] rather+ (*alla*), +as regards your+ (*tu*) +humblemindedness+, your view of yourselves learnt at the feet of your Saviour, +reckon[5] each other superior to yourselves+; as assuredly you will do, with a logic true to the soul, when each sees himself, the personality he knows best, in the light of eternal holiness

Ver. 4. and love. +Not to your own+ interests +look+ (*skopountes*), +each circle of you, but each circle[6] to those+

Ver. 5. +of others also. Have this mind+ (*phroneite*) in +you+, this moral attitude in each soul, +which+ was, and is,[7] +also in Christ Jesus+, (in that eternal Messiah whom I name already with His human Name, JESUS; for in the will of His Father, and in the unity of His own Person, it was as it were His Name already

Ver. 6. from everlasting,) +who in God's manifested Being[8] subsisting+,[9] *seeming* divine, because He *was* divine, in the full sense of Deity, in that eternal world, +reckoned it no plunderer's prize[10] to be on an equality with God+;[11] no, He viewed His possession of the fulness of the Eternal Nature as securely and inalienably His own, and *so* He dealt with it for our sakes with a sublime and *restful* remembrance of others; far from thinking of it as for Himself alone, as one who claimed it unlawfully would have done,

Ver. 7. +He rather (*alla*) made Himself void by His own act+,[12] void of the manifestation and exercise of Deity as it was His on the throne,[13] +taking[14] Bond-servant's+ (*doulou*) +manifested being+ (*morphê*), that is to say, the veritable Human Nature which, as a creaturely nature, is essentially bound to the service of the Creator, the _bond_service of the Father; +coming to be+, becoming, *genomenos*, +in men's similitude+, so truly human as not only to be but *to seem* Man, accepting all the conditions involved in a truly human *exterior*,

Ver. 8. "pleased *as Man with men* to appear." +And+ then, further, +being found+, as He offered Himself to view, +in respect of guise+ (*schêati*), in respect of outward shape, and habit, and address, +as Man+, He went further, He stooped yet lower, even from Humanity to Death; +He humbled Himself, in becoming obedient+,[15] obedient to Him whose Bondservant He now was as Man, +to the length[16] of death, aye+ (*de*), +death of Cross+, that death of unimaginable pain and of utmost shame, the death which to the Jew was the symbol of the curse of God upon the victim, and to the Roman was a horror of degradation which should be "far not only from the bodies but from the imaginations of citizens of Rome."[17]

So He came, and so He suffered, because "He

Ver. 9. looked to the interests of others." +Wherefore also God+, His God (*ho theos*), +supremely exalted Him+, in His Resurrection and Ascension, +and conferred upon Him+, as a gift of infinite love and approval (*echarisato*), +the Name which is above every name+; THE NAME, unique and glorious; the Name Supreme, the I AM; to be His Name now, not only as He is from eternity, the everlasting Son of the Father, but as He became also in time, the suffering and risen Saviour of sinners.[18] In His whole character and work He is invested now with the transcendent glory and greatness of divine dignity; every thought of the suffering Manhood is steeped in the fact that He who, looking on the things of others, came down to bear it, is now enthroned where only the Absolute and Eternal King

Ver. 10. can sit; +so that in the Name of Jesus+,[19] in presence of the revealed majesty of Him who bears, as Man, the human personal Name, Jesus, +every knee should bow+, as the prophet (Isa. xlv. 23) foretells, +of things celestial, and terrestrial, and subterranean+, of all created existence, in its heights and depths; spirits, men, and every other creature; all bowing, each in their way, to the *imperium* of the exalted Jesus,

Ver. 11. JEHOVAH-JESUS; +and that every tongue should confess+, with the confessing of adoring, praising, worship (*exomologêsêtai*), +that Jesus Christ is+ nothing less than +Lord+, in the supreme and ultimate sense of that mighty word, +to God the Father's glory+. For the worship given to "His Own Son" (Rom. viii. 32), whose Nature is one with His, whose glories flow eternally from Him, is praise given to Him.[20]

So closes one of the most conspicuous and magnificent of the dogmatic utterances of the New Testament. Let us consider it for a few moments from that point of view alone. We have here a chain of assertions about our Lord Jesus Christ, made within some thirty years of His death at Jerusalem; made in the open day of public Christian intercourse, and made (every reader must feel this) not in the least in the manner of controversy, of assertion against difficulties and denials, but in the tone of a settled, common, and most living certainty. These assertions give us on the one hand the fullest possible assurance that He is Man, Man in nature, in circumstances and experience, and particularly in the sphere of relation to God the Father. But they also assure us, in precisely the same tone, and in a way which is equally vital to the argument in hand, that He is as genuinely Divine as He is genuinely Human. Did He "come to be in Bondservant's Form"? And does the word Form, *morphê*, there, unless the glowing argument is to run as cold as ice, mean, as it ought to mean, reality in manifestation, fact in sight, a Manhood perfectly real, carrying with it a veritable creaturely {98} obligation (*douleia*) to God? But He was also, antecedently, "in God's Form." And there too therefore we are to understand, unless the wonderful words are to be robbed of all their living power, that He who came to be Man, and to seem Man, in an antecedent state of His blessed Being was God, and seemed God. And His "becoming to be" one with us in that mysterious but genuine Bondservice was the free and conscious choice of His eternal Will, His eternal Love, in the glory of the Throne. "When He came on earth abased" He was no Victim of a secret and irresistible destiny, such as that which in the Stoic's theology swept the Gods of Olympus to their hour of change and extinction as surely as it swept men to ultimate annihilation. "*He made Himself* void," with all the foresight and with all the freewill which can be exercised upon the Throne where the Son is in the Form of the Eternal Nature. Such is the Christology of the passage in its aspect towards Deity.

Then in regard of our beloved Lord's Manhood, its implications assure us that the perfect genuineness of that Manhood, which could not be expressed in a term more profound and complete than this same *morphê doulou*, Form of Bondservant, leaves us yet perfectly sure that He who chose to be Bondservant is to us only all the more, even in His Manhood, LORD. Was it not His own prescient choice to be true Man? And was it not His choice with a prescient and infallible regard to "the things of others," to "us men and our salvation"? Then we may be sure that, whatever is meant by the "made Himself void," *heauton ekenôsen*, which describes His Incarnation here, one thing it could never possibly mean——a "Kenôsis" which could hurt or distort His absolute fitness to guide and bless us whom He came to save. That awful and benignant "Exinanition" placed Him indeed on the creaturely level in regard of the reality of human experience of growth, and human capacity for suffering. But never for one moment did it, could it, make Him other than the absolute and infallible Master and Guide of His redeemed.

We are beset at the present day, on many sides, with speculations about the "Kenôsis" of the Lord which in some cases anyhow have it for their manifest goal to justify the thought that He condescended to be fallible; that He "made Himself void" of such knowledge as should protect Him from mistaken statements about, for example, the history, quality, and authority of the Old Testament Scriptures. I have said once and again elsewhere[21] that such an application of the "made Himself void," *heauton ekenôsen*, of this passage (from which alone we get the word Kenôsis for the Incarnation) is essentially beside the mark. The Kenôsis here is a very definite thing, as we see when we read the Greek. It is just this—the taking of "Bondservant's Form." It is—the becoming the absolute Human Bondservant of the Father. And the Absolute Bondservant must exercise a perfect Bond-service. And this will mean, amidst all else that it may mean, a perfect conveyance of the Supreme Master's mind in the delivery of His message. "*He whom God hath sent, speaketh the words of God.*" The Kenôsis itself (as St Paul meant it) is nothing less than the guarantee of the Infallibility. It says neither yes nor no to the question, Was our Redeemer, as Man, "in the days of His flesh," omniscient? It says a profound and decisive yes to the question, Is our Redeemer, as Man, "in the days of His flesh," to be absolutely trusted as the Truth in every syllable of assertion which He was actually pleased to make? *"He whom God hath sent, speaketh the words of God."*

The dogmatic treasures of this wonderful passage are by no means exhausted, even when we have drawn from it what it can say to us about the glory of the Lord Christ Jesus. But it is not possible to follow the research further, here and now; this imperfect indication of the main teachings about Him must be enough.

But now, in closing, let us remember for our blessing how this passage of didactic splendour comes in. It is no lecture in the abstract. As we have seen, it is not in the least a controversial assertion. It is simply part of an argument to the heart. St Paul is not here, as elsewhere in his Epistles, combating an error of faith; he is pleading for a life of love. He has full in view the temptations which threatened to mar the happy harmony of Christian fellowship at Philippi. His longing is that they should be "of one accord, of one mind"; and that in order to that blessed end they should each forget himself and remember others. He appeals to them by many motives; by their common share in Christ, and in the Spirit, and by the simple plea of their affection for himself. But then—there is one plea more; it is "the mind that was in Christ Jesus," when "for us men and for our salvation He came down from heaven, and was made Man, and suffered for us." Here was at once model and motive for the Philippian saints; for Euodia, and Syntyche, and every individual, and every group. Nothing short of the "mind" of the Head must be the "mind" of the member; and then the glory of the Head (so it is implied) shall be shed hereafter upon the member too: "I will grant to him to sit with Me in My throne, even as I also overcame, and am set down with My Father in His throne."

What a comment is this upon that fallacy of religious thought which would dismiss Christian doctrine to the region of theorists and dreamers, in favour of Christian "life"! Christian doctrine, rightly so called, is simply the articulate statement, according to the Scriptures, of eternal and vital facts, that we may live by them. The passage before us is charged to the brim with the doctrine of the Person and the Natures of Christ. And why? It is in order that the Christian, tempted to a self-asserting life, may "look upon the things of others," for the reason that this supreme Fact, his Saviour, is in fact thus and thus, and did in fact think and act thus and thus for His people. Without the

45

facts, which are the doctrine, we might have had abundant rhetoric in St Paul's appeal for unselfishness and harmony; but where would have been the mighty lever for the affections and the will?

Oh reason of reasons, argument of arguments—the LORD JESUS CHRIST! Nothing in Christianity lies really outside Him. His Person and His Work embody all its dogmatic teaching. His Example, "His Love which passeth knowledge," is the sum and life of all its morality. Well has it been said that the whole Gospel message is conveyed to us sinners in those three words, "Looking unto Jesus." Is it pardon we need, is it acceptance, free as the love of God, holy as His law? We find it, we possess it, "looking unto Jesus" crucified. Is it power we need, victory and triumph over sin, capacity and willingness to witness and to suffer in a world which loves Him not at all? We find it, we possess it, it possesses us, as we "look unto Jesus" risen and reigning, for us on the Throne, with us in the soul. Is it rule and model that we want, not written on the stones of Horeb only, but "on the fleshy tables of the heart"? We find it, we receive it, we yield ourselves up to it, as we "look unto Jesus" in His path of love, from the Throne to the Cross, from the Cross to the Throne, till the Spirit inscribes that law upon our inmost wills.

Be ever more and more to us, Lord Jesus Christ, in all Thy answer, to our boundless needs. Let us "sink to no second cause." Let us come to Thee. Let us yield to Thee. Let us follow Thee. Present Thyself evermore to us as literally our all in all. And so through a blessed fellowship in Thy wonderful humiliation we shall partake for ever hereafter in the exaltations of Thy glory, which is the glory of immortal love.

[1] *Koinûnia pneumatos*: "participation in the Spirit"; sharing and sharing alike in the grace and power of the Holy Ghost. I venture to render *pneumatos* as if it were *tou Pneumatos*, having regard to the great parallel passage, 2 Cor. xiii. 14, *he koinônia tou hagiou Pneumatos*. With a word so great and conspicuous as *pneuma* it is impossible to decide by the mere absence of the article that the reference is not to *the* (personal) Spirit. *Kurios, Theos, Christos*, are continually given without the article where the reference is definite; because they are words whose greatness tends of itself to define the reference, unless context withstands. *Pneuma* in the N. T. is to some extent a parallel case with these.

[2] *Ina ... phronute*: my English is obviously a mere paraphrase here. More exactly we may render, "make full my joy, so as to be," etc.; words which come to much the same effect, but are less true to our common idioms.

[3] *To en phronountes*: a difficult phrase to render quite adequately. We may paraphrase it either as above, or, "possessed with the idea, or sentiment, of unity." But the paraphrase above seems most satisfactory in view of the

similar phrase just before, *to auto phronête*. This phrase seems to echo that, only in a stronger and less usual form. The thought thus will be not so much of unity as the object of thought or feeling as of unity as (so to speak) the substance or spirit of it.

[4] *Kata eritheian*: my long paraphrase attempts to give the suggestion that the *eritheia* might be either purely individual self-assertion or the *animus* of a clique.

[5] *Hêgoumenoi*: the participle practically does the work of an imperative. See Rom. xii. for a striking chain of examples of this powerful and intelligible idiom.

[6] *Hekastoi*, not *hekastos*, should probably be read in the first clause here, and certainly in the second. By Greek idiom, the plural gives the thought of a *collective* unity under "each."

[7] The Greek gives no verb. I have written "was, and is," in the paraphrase, because the *limitation* of the reference of our blessed Lord's *phronêma* to the pre-incarnate past is not expressed in the Greek.

[8] *En morphê*: morphê is imperfectly represented by our common use of the word "form," which stands often even in contrast to "reality." *Morphê* is *reality in manifestation*.

[9] *Uparchôn*: R.V. margin, "originally being." The word lends itself to such a reference, but not so invariably as to allow us to press it here.

[10] *Arpagmon*: the word is extremely rare, found here only in the Greek Scriptures, and once only in secular Greek. Strictly, by form (*-mon*), it should mean, "*a process* of plunder" rather than "an object of plunder" (*-ma*). But parallel cases forbid us to press this. The A.V. rendering here suggests the thought that our Lord "thought it no usurpation to be equal with God, *and yet* made Himself void," etc. But surely the thought is rather, "*and so* made Himself void." So sure was His claim that, so to speak, with a sublime *un-anxiety*, while with an infinite sacrifice, He made Himself void.

[11] *Isa Theô*: the neuter plural calls attention rather to the Characteristics than to the Personality.—Through this whole passage we cannot too distinctly remember that it occurs in the Scriptures, and in the writings of one who was trained in the strictest school of Pharisaic Monotheism. *St Paul* was not the man to use such terms of his Saviour and Master had he not seen in Him nothing less than the very "Fellow of JEHOVAH" (Zech. xiii. 7).

[12] *Eauton ekeôse*: Heauton is slightly emphatic by position; I attempt to convey this by the words "by His own act."

[13] See further below, pp. 98, etc. [Transcriber's note: page 98 is indicated in this text with "{98}".]

[14] *Labôn*: the aorist participle, in Greek idiom, unites itself closely in thought with the aorist verb *ekenôse* just previous. The resulting idea is not "He made Himself void, and then took," but "He made Himself void *by taking.*" The "Exinanition" was, in fact, just this—*the taking the form of the doulos*: neither less nor more.

[15] Note again the aorist verb and aorist participle: *etapeinôse ... genomenos.*

[16] The Greek, *mechri thanatou*, makes it plain that the Lord did not *obey death* but *obeyed the Father* so utterly as even to die.

[17] Cicero, *pro Rabirio*, c. 5.

[18] Bishop Lightfoot has well vindicated this reference of the *onoma* here. I venture to refer the reader also to my commentary on Philippians, in *The Cambridge Bible for Schools and Colleges.*

[19] Not "the Name Jesus," but "the Name of, belonging to, Jesus." The grammar admits either rendering, but the context, if I explain it aright, is decisive. "The Name" is still the Supreme Name, JEHOVAH, as just above. —"*In* the Name" should be explained, in view of the context, not of worship *through* but worship yielded *to* the Name. See Lightfoot for examples of this usage.

[20] Chrysostom brings this great truth nobly out in his homiletic comments here (*Hom.* vii. on Philippians, ch. 4): "A mighty proof it is of the Father's power, and goodness, and wisdom, that He hath begotten such a Son, a Son nowise inferior in goodness and wisdom ... like Him in all things, Fatherhood alone excepted." Nothing but the orthodox Creed, with its harmonious truths of the proper Godhead and proper Filiation of the Lord Christ, can possibly satisfy *the whole* of the apostolic language about His infinite glory on the one hand and His relation to the Father on the other.

[21] In my *Veni Creator* and *To my Younger Brethren*, and more recently in a University Sermon quoted at the close of a little book published Easter, 1896, by Seeley: *Prayers and Promises.*

"Make my life a bright outshining
  Of Thy life, that all may see
Thine own resurrection power
Mightily shewn forth in me;
Ever let my heart become
Yet more consciously Thy home."

MISS J. S. PIGOTT.

# THE LORD'S POWER IN THE DISCIPLE'S LIFE

"O Jesus Christ, grow Thou in me,
 And all things else recede;
My heart be daily nearer Thee,
 From sin be daily freed.

"More of Thy glory let me see,
 Thou Holy, Wise, and True;
I would Thy living image be
 In joy and sorrow too."
        H. B. SMITH, *from the German of* C. LAVATER.


## CHAPTER VI

### THE LORD'S POWER IN THE DISCIPLE'S LIFE

PHILIPPIANS ii. 12-18

"Your own salvation"—Stars in the midnight sky—Truth and holiness—The atonement and the indwelling—Mystery and need of the indwelling—Indifference in God—Spiritual power shewn in love—Aggression and witness—The witnesses and the martyr

We have just followed the Apostle as he has followed the Saviour of sinners from the Throne to the Cross, and from the Cross to the Throne. And we have remembered the moral motive of that wonderful paragraph of spiritual revelation. It was written not to occupy the mind merely, or to elevate it, but to bring the believer's heart into a delightful subjection to Him who "pleased not Himself," till the Lord should be reflected in the self-forgetting life of His follower.

In the passage now opening before us we find St Paul's thought still working in continuity with this argument. He has still in his heart the risks of friction at Philippi, and the need of meeting them in the power of the Lord's example. This will come out particularly in the fourteenth and fifteenth verses, where he deprecates "murmurings and disputings," and pleads for a life of pure, sweet light and love. But the line of appeal, though continuous, is now somewhat altered in its direction. The divine greatness of the love of the Incarnation has, during his treatment of it, filled him with an intense and profound recollection of the greatness of the Christian's connexion with his God, and of the sacred awfulness of his responsibility, and of the fulness of his resources. So the appeal now is not merely to be like-minded, and to be watchful for unity. He asks them now to use fully for a life of holiness the mighty fact of their possession of an Indwelling God in Christ. The details of precept are as it were absorbed for the time into the glorious power and principle—only to reappear the more largely and lastingly in the resulting life.

Ver. 12. +So, my beloved ones+, (he often introduces his most practical appeals with this term of affection: see for example 1 Cor. x. 14, xv. 58; 2 Cor. vii. 1,) +just as you always obeyed+[1] me, obey me now. +Not+ (*mê*, the *imperative* negative) as in my presence only, influenced by that immediate contact and intercourse, +but now much more in my absence+, ("much more," as my absence throws you more directly on your resources in the Lord,) +work out+, develope, +your own salvation+, your own spiritual safety, health, and joy, +with fear and trembling+; not with the tortures of misgiving, not driven by a shrinking dread of your gracious God, but drawn by a tender reverence and solemn watchfulness, lest you should grieve the eternal Love. Yes, "work out *your own* salvation"; do not depend upon *me*; take *your own* souls in hand, in a faith and love which look, without the least earthly intermediation, straight to GOD and to Him alone.[2] For indeed He is near to you; far nearer than ever a Paul could be; "a very present help," for

Ver. 13. your safety, and for your holiness. +For God it is who is effecting+ (*energôs*) +in you+, in your very being, in "the first springs of thought and will," +both your+ (*to*) +willing and your effecting+, your carrying out the willing, +for His+ (*tês*) +good pleasure's sake+; in order to the accomplishment through you of all His holy purposes. Here, in this wonderful immanence, this divine indwelling, and in its living, operative power, you will find reason enough alike for the "fear and trembling" of deepest reverence, and for the calm resourceful confidence of those who can, if need be, "walk alone," as regards dependence upon even an apostolic friend beside them. Live then as those who carry about with them the very life and power of God in Christ. And what will that life be? A life of spiritual ostentation? Nay, the beautiful and

Ver. 14. gentle opposite to it. +Do all things without+, apart from (*chôris*), in a definite isolation from, +murmurings and disputes+, thoughts and utterances of discontent and self-assertion towards one another, grudgings of others' claims, and contentions for your

Ver. 15. own; +so that you may become+ (*genêsthe*), what in full realization you scarcely yet are, +unblamable and simple+ (*akeraioi*, "unadulterated"), single-hearted, because self-forgetting; +God's children+ (*tekna*), shewing

51

what they are by the unmistakable *family-likeness* of holy love; +blameless+ as such, true to your character; +in the midst of a race+ (*geneas*) +crooked and distorted+, the members of a world whose will always crosses the will of God who is Love; +among whom you are appearing+, like stars which come out in the gloom, +as luminaries+ (*phôstêres*), light-bearers, kindled by the Lord of Light, +in the world+; in which you dwell; not of it, but in it, walking up and down "before the sons of men" (Ps. xxxi. 19), that they may see, and seek,

Ver. 16. your blessed Secret; +holding out+ (*epechontes*[3]), as those who offer a boon for acceptance, +the word of life+, the Gospel, with its secret of eternal life in Christ; at once telling and commending His message; +to afford me+, even me (*emoi*), +exultation, in view of+ (*eis*) +Christ's Day+, in anticipation of what I shall feel then; +because not in vain did I run, nor in vain did I toil+.[4] But let me not speak of "toil" as if I sighed over a hard lot, or wished to suffer less on your behalf.

Ver. 17. +Nay, even if I am being poured out as a drink-offering+ (*spendomai*) +on the sacrifice and ritual+ (*leitourgia*) +of your faith+—on you, so to speak, as you in faith offer yourselves a living sacrifice to God[5]—+I rejoice, and I congratulate+ (*sugchairô*) +you all+, on your faith and holiness, for which it was well worth my while to die as your helper and example. +And in+

Ver. 18. +the same way+ (*to de aûto*) +do you too rejoice, and congratulate me+,[6] as true partners with me in the martyr-spirit and its joys.

Here let us pause in our paraphrasing version, and sit down as it were to gather up and weigh some of the treasures we have found.

i. We have had before us, in the whole passage, that ever-recurring lesson, Holiness in the Truth, as Truth—"the Truth as it is in Jesus"—is the living secret of Holiness. We have still in our ears the celestial music, infinitely sweet and full, of the great paragraph of the Incarnation, the journey of the Lord of Love from glory to glory by the way of the awful Cross. May we not now give ourselves awhile wholly to reverie, and feast upon the divine poetry at our leisure? Not so; the immediate sequel is—that we are to be holy. We are *to act* in the light and wonder of so vast an act of love, in the wealth and resource of "so great salvation." We are to set spiritually to work. We are to learn that all-important lesson in religion, the holy and humble energy and independence which come to the man who "knows whom he has believed," and is aware that he possesses "all spiritual blessing" (Eph. i. 3) in Him. We are to rise up and, if need be, walk alone, alone of human help, in the certainty that Christ has died for us, and reigns for us, and in us. Our Paul may be far away in some distant Rome, and we may sorely miss him. But we have at hand Jesus Christ, who "took Bondservant's Form," and obeyed even unto death for us, and who is on the eternal throne for us, and who lives within us by His Spirit. Looking upon Him in the glory of His Person and His Work, we are not only to wonder, not only even to worship; we are to work; to "work out" our spiritual blessings[7] into a life which shall be full of Him, and in which we shall indeed be "saved" ourselves, and help others around us to their salvation. In the "fear and trembling" of those who feel the blissful awfulness of an eternal Presence, we are to set ourselves, with the inexhaustible diligence of hope, to the business of the spiritual life. We are to bring all the treasures of a manifested and possessed Redeemer to bear upon the passing hour, and to let Him be seen in us, "Christ our Life," always formative and empowering.

ii. We have here in particular that deep secret of the Gospel, unspeakably precious to the soul which indeed longs to be holy—the Indwelling of God in the believer. It here appears in close and significant connexion with the revelation of the love and work of the Incarnate and Atoning Lord; as if to remind us without more words that He who gave Himself for us did so not only to release us (blessed be His Name) from an infinite peril, from the eternal prison and death of a violated law, but yet more that He might bring His rescued ones into an unspeakable nearness in Him to God. His was no *mere* compassion, which could set a guilty captive free. It was eternal love, which could not be content without nearness to its object, without union with it, without a dwelling in the very heart by faith. As if it was a matter of course in the plan of God, St Paul passes from the Cross and the Glory of Jesus to the Indwelling of God in the Christian, and to all the rest and all the power which that Indwelling is to bring.

"It is God who is working in you, effecting alike your willing and your working; for the sake of His good pleasure." These are words of deep mystery. They contain matter which has exercised the closest thought of some of the greatest thinkers of the Church. *Operatur in nobis velle*; "He worketh in us to will." How is this to be reconciled with the reality, and in that sense the freedom, of the human will? What relation does it bear to human responsibility, and to the call to watch, and pray, and labour? Very soon, over such questions, we have, in the phrase of the Rabbis, to "teach our tongue to say, *I do not know*." But the words appear *in this context* with a purpose perfectly simple and practical, whatever be their more remote and hidden indications. They do indeed intimate to us a reality and energy in the divine sovereignty which may well correct those dreams of self-salvation which man is so ready to dream. But their more immediate purpose is as simple as it is profound. It is on the one hand to solemnize the disciple with the remembrance of such an inward *Presence*, and on the other hand to make him always glad and ready, recollecting that such an inward *Power* is there, altogether for his highest good, and altogether in the line of the eternal purpose (*eudokia*). For the while at least let us drop out of sight all hard questions of theoretical adjustment between the finite will and the Infinite, and rest quite simply in that thought:—God is in me, working the willing and the doing. The willing is genuine, and is mine. The working is genuine, and is mine. *My* will chooses Him, and *my* activity labours for Him; both are real, and are personally mine. But He is at the back; He is at "the pulse of the machine"; I, His personal creature, am held in no less a hold than His, to be moulded and to be employed; His implement, His limb.

Not very long ago I was in conversation with a young but deeply thoughtful Christian, who, placed on a difficult social height, was seeking with deep desire not only to "follow the Lamb whithersoever He goeth" but to lead others similarly circumstanced to do the same. I was struck with the strong consciousness which possessed that heart, that the religious life must inevitably be a weary and exhausting effort on any other condition than this —"God working in us, to will and to do." "Ah, they all say that it is so hard; no one can really do it; no one can keep it up. But we must speak to them about the indwelling Spirit of God, about the Lord's power in us; *then* they will find that it is possible, and is happy."

*Chôris emou*—"isolated from Me (John xv. 5)—*ye can do nothing*"; and what seems our "doing" will, in such isolation, be only too sorely felt to be a weary toil. But let us accept it as true, at the foot of the atoning Cross, that the Indwelling of God in Christ is as much a fact as our pardon and adoption in Him, and we shall know something of the blessed life. Only, we must not only accept it as true, but use it. *"Work out*—for it is God who is *working in* you."*

And, let us remember it once more, we shall learn in that quiet School not only a restful energy but also that holy independence (*tên heautôn sôtêrian*) which is, in its place, the priceless gain of the Christian. Our spiritual life is indeed intended to be social in its issues—but not at its root. We accept and thankfully use every assistance given us by our Lord's care, as we live our life in His Church; yet our life, as to its source, is to be still "hidden with Christ in God." We are to be so related to Him, in faith, that our soul's health, growth, gladness, shall depend not on the presence of even a St Paul at our side, but on the presence of God in our hearts. Let us cherish this blessed certainty, and develope it into experience, in these strange days of unrest and drift. That secret independence will do anything but isolate us from our fellows. It will make us fit, as nothing else could make us, to be their strength and light, in truest sympathy, in kindest insight, in the fullest sense of loving partnership. But we must learn independence in God if we would be fully serviceable to man.

iii. We have in this passage one of the richest and most beautiful expressions found in the whole New Testament of that great principle, that at the very heart of a true life of holiness there needs to lie the law of holy kindness. The connexion of thought between ver. 13 and ver. 14 is deeply suggestive here. In ver. 13 we have the power and wonder of the operative Indwelling of God. In ver. 14 we have depicted the true conduct of the subjects of the Indwelling; and it shines with the sweet light of humility and gentleness. It is a life whose hidden power, which is nothing less than divine, comes out first and most in the absence of the grudging, self-asserting spirit; in a watchful consistency and simplicity; in the manifestation of the *child*-character, as the believer moves about "in the midst of" the hard and most unchildlike conditions of an unregenerate world. There is to be action as well as patience; this we shall see presently. The disciple is to be aggressive, in the right way, as well as submissive. But the first and deepest characteristic of his wonderful new life is to be the submission of himself to others, "in the Lord, and in the power of His might." We have this aspect of practical holiness presented to us often in the general teaching of the New Testament; but seldom is it so explicitly connected as it is here with that other spiritual fact, the presence in us of the divine *power*. Perhaps our best parallels come from the two other Epistles of the Roman Captivity, Ephesians and Colossians. In Ephesians, the third chapter closes with the astonishing prayer that the Christian (the everyday Christian, be it remembered) may be, through the Indwelling of Christ, "filled unto all the fulness of God"; and then the fourth chapter begins at once with the appeal to him to live "*therefore*" a life of "all lowliness, meekness, longsuffering, and forbearance in love." In Colossians we have the same sequence of thought in one noble sentence (ver. 11) of the first chapter: "Strengthened with all strength, according to the might of His glory, *unto all patience and longsuffering, with joy*."[8] In all three passages comes out the same deep and beautiful suggestion. "The Lord is not in the wind" so much as in "the still small voice." Omnipotent Love, in its blessed immanence in the believer's soul, shews its presence and power most of all in a life *of love* around. It is to come out not only in self-sacrificing energy but in the open sympathies of an affectionate heart, in the "soft answer," in the generous first thought for the interests of others—in short, in the whole character of 1 Cor. xiii. The spiritual "power" which runs rather in the direction of harshness and isolation, which expends itself rather in censures than in "longsuffering, gentleness, goodness, and meekness," is not the kind of "power" which most accords with the apostolic idea. Nothing which violates the plain precepts of the law of love can take a true part in that heavenly harmony.

"On earth, as in the holy place,

Nothing is great but charity." [9]

iv. Meanwhile the "charity" of the saints is not by any means the mere amiability which makes itself pleasant to every one, and forgets the solemn fact that we who believe are the servants of a Master whom the world knows not, the messengers of a King against whom it is in revolt. The Philippian disciple was to renounce the spirit of unkindness, of self; he was to live *isolated* from (*chôris*) "murmurings and disputings." But he was not to hide the sacred Light, for the sake of so-called peace, from the world around. He was to "hold out the word of life"; confessing his blessed Lord as the life of his own soul, and so commending Him to the souls of his fellows. He was to make this a part of his very existence and its activities. As truly as it was to be his habit to live a life of sweet and winning consistency, it was to be his habit to offer (*epechein*) the water of life to the parched hearts around him, the lamp of glory to the dark and bewildered whom he encountered upon the difficult road. The truth and beauty of a *life* possessed by Christ was to be the basis of his witnessing activities. But the witness was to be articulate, not merely implied; he was to "hold out *the word* (*logon*) of life"; he was to seize occasion to "give *a reason* (*logon*) of the hope that was in him, with meekness and fear" (1 Pet. iii. 15). To be, in his way, an evangelist was to be one main function of his life. In benignant and gracious conduct he was to be as a "luminary" (*phôstêr*), moving calm and bright in the dark hemisphere of the world. But he was to be a voice as well as a star. He was not only to shine; he was to speak.

Here is one of the passages, by the way, in which the Apostle assumes, and stimulates, the "missionary consciousness" of the converts. It is remarkable that neither he nor his brethren have much to say in the Epistles about the duty of enterprises of evangelization, as laid upon all believers. The stress of their appeals is directed above all things on the supreme importance of holiness, at any cost, in common life. But a passage like this shews us how entirely they take it for granted all the time that the Churches would never concentrate themselves upon merely their own Christian life; they would go out continually, with the beauty of holiness and with "the word of life," to bring the wanderers in, and to extend the knowledge of the blessed Name. So, and so only, would their Apostle feel, in his prison at Rome, that his "running" (*edramon*) on the great circuit of his evangelistic journeys, and his pastoral "toil" (*ekopiasa*) for the souls of his converts, had not been thrown "into the void" (*eis to kenon*).

So, and so only, would his life and death of sacrifice for them be crowned with its perfect joy. Let him see his beloved converts living and speaking as indeed the Lord's *witnesses*, and then with what inward "gladness" (*chairein*), with what a call for "congratulation" (*sugchairein*) on their part, would he go out to death as the Lord's *martyr*!

[1] *Upêkousate*: the aorist. It gathers into one thought the whole recollection of his work at Philippi.

[2] "There is not the slightest contradiction here to the profound truth of the Justification by Faith only; that is to say, only for the merit's sake of the Redeemer, appropriated by submissive trust; that justification whose sure issue is glorification (Rom. viii. 30). It is an instance of independent lines converging on one goal. From one point of view, that of justifying merit, man is glorified because of Christ's work alone, applied to his case through faith alone. From another point, that of qualifying capacity, and of preparation for the Lord's individual welcome (Matt. xxv. 21; Rom. ii. 7), man is glorified as the issue of a process of work and training, in which in a true sense he is himself operant, though grace lies below the whole operation." (Note on this verse in *The Cambridge Bible for Schools and Colleges*).

[3] It is possible to render *logon xôeê epechontes*, "serving as life (to the world)." But it is unlikely. See Philippians in *The Cambridge Greek Testament*, Appendix.

[4] The aorists obviously are anticipatory; giving the review of the past as he will then make it. Cp. e.g. *kathôs epegnôsthên*, 1 Cor. xiii. 12.

[5] "He views the Philippians, in their character of consecrated believers (cp. Rom. xii. 1), as a holocaust to God; and upon that sacrifice the drink-offering, the outpoured wine, is his own life-blood, his martyrdom for the Gospel which he has preached to them. Cp. Num. xv. 5 for the Mosaic libation, *oinon eis spondên … poisête epi tês holokautôseôs.* Lightfoot thinks that a reference to pagan libations is more likely in a letter to a Gentile mission. But surely St Paul familiarized all his converts with Old Testament symbolism. And *his own* mind was of course full of it (Note here in *The Cambridge Greek Testament for Schools*).—This and Rom. xv. 16 are the only two passages where St Paul connects the language of "sacerdotalism" with the distinctive work of the Christian ministry; and both passages speak obviously in the tone of figure and, so to say, poetry.

*[6] Chairete: sugchairete.* The form leaves us free to render either *indicative* or *imperative.* But the latter is most likely in the context.

[7] *Sôtêria* must here include not only final glory but the whole blessing possessed now and always in the *Sôtêr.*

[8] "Observe the holy paradox of the thought here. The fulness of divine power in the saints is to result primarily not in 'doing some great thing' but in enduring and forbearing, with heavenly joy of heart. The paradox points to one deep characteristic of the Gospel, which prepares the Christian for service by the way of a true abnegation of himself as his own strength and his own aim." (Note on Col. i. 11 in *The Cambridge Bible*).

[9] A. Vinet, *Hymn on the Crucifixion*, translated by C. W. Moule.

"O thou who makest souls to shine
  With light from brighter worlds above,
And droppest glistening dew divine
  On all who seek a Saviour's love,

"Do Thou Thy benediction give
  On all who teach, on all who learn,
That all Thy Church may holier live,
  And every lamp more brightly burn.

\* \* \* \* \*

"If thus, good Lord, Thy grace be giv'n
Our glory meets us ere we die;
Before we upward pass to heav'n
We taste our immortality."
    J. ARMSTRONG.

# TIMOTHEUS AND EPAPHRODITUS

"Puisse la même foi qui consola leur vie
Nous ouvrir les sentiers que leurs pas ont pressés,
Et, dirigeant nos pieds vers la sainte patrie
Où leur bonheur s'accroit de leurs travaux passés,
Nous rendre ces objets de tendresse et d'envie
Qui ne sont pas perdus, mais nous ont devancés."
A. VINET


## CHAPTER VII

**TIMOTHEUS AND EPAPHRODITUS**

PHILIPPIANS ii. 19-30

Epaphroditus—The variety of Scripture—Contrasts in context—Henry Martyn's letter—"The human element"—"His letters I have read"—The two aspects of Scripture—Divine messages in human context—"Together with them"

Ver. 19. +But I hope in the Lord Jesus+, with an expectation conditioned by my union with Him in all things, and with you in Him, +promptly to send to you Timotheus,[1] that I too+, I as well as you, who will of course be gladdened by his presence, +may be of good cheer, getting+, through him, +a knowledge+ (*gnous*) +of your circumstances+ (*ta peri humôn*). I send him, and not

Ver. 20. another, +for I have+—at hand, and free to move—+no one equal-souled+ with him,[2] +one who+ (*hootis*) +will genuinely take anxious care about your circumstances+; the "care" which is not a weary burthen, better cast upon the Lord (iv. 6), but a sacred charge, undertaken in and for Him, and absorbing all the

Ver. 21. thought. +For all of them+ (*oi pantes*), all from whom I could in this case select, +are bent on+ (*xêtousi*: cp. Col. iii. 1) +their own interests, not the interests of Jesus Christ+; they plead excuses which indicate a preference of their own ease, or reputation, or affections, to a matter manifestly and wholly HIS.

Ver. 22. +But the test through which he+, Timotheus, +passed+ (*tên dokimên autou*) you remember (*ginôskete*, "you recognize," as you look back); you know +that as child with father+ so +he with me+, in closest companionship and sympathy, +did bondservice[3] for the Gospel+, *eis to euaggelion*, "*unto it*," for the furtherance

Ver. 23. of its enterprise and message. +So him then+ (*touton men oun*[4]) +I hope to send, immediately upon+ (*hôs an ... exautês*) +my getting a view of+ (*apidô*) +my circumstances+, my position with regard to my trial

Ver. 24. and its result. +But+ (though I thus allude to external uncertainties) +I feel sure, in the Lord+, in the light of union and communion with Him, +that I too in person shall speedily arrive+, in the track of this my messenger and forerunner.

Ver. 25. +But I count[5] it obligatory+ (*anagkaion*), and not merely a matter for hopes and personal satisfaction, +to send to you+, as I now do, in charge of this Letter, another person, +Epaphroditus, my brother, fellow-worker, and fellow-soldier+, a man who has toiled and contended at my very side for the Lord and against the Enemy, +while he is+ also +your missionary and ministrant[6] for my need+. Yes, I feel that I *ought*

Ver. 26. to send him, and to send him *now*; +since he has been suffering from home-sickness for[7] all of you+, (all, without exception; his affection knows no party or partiality,) +and from the distraction+ (*adêmonôn*) of over-wrought feeling, because you have heard that he

Ver. 27. fell ill[8] (*êsthenêse*). +And+ so it was; +for he did fall ill, almost fatally+ (*paraplêsion thanatô*). +But our+ (*ho*) +God pitied him+, sparing him the grief of broken hopes and purposes in the Lord's work on earth, and the grief of being a cause of tears to you; +and not only him but also me, that I might not have[9] sorrow upon sorrow+. For had he died, I should have had a sore bereavement, and the sad consciousness that you, in a loving effort for my benefit, had lost a beloved friend; and all this added to, heaped upon (*epi c. acc.*), the antecedent pain of my captivity and the trials which it involves.

Ver. 28. +With the more earnestness therefore I have sent him,[10] that seeing him you may be glad again, and that I may feel less sorrow+, finding my imprisonment, and also my loss of this dear friend's company, softened to my heart by the thought of your joy in

Ver. 29. welcoming him back. +Receive him therefore in the Lord+, in all the union and sympathy due to your common share in Him, +with all gladness, and+

Ver. 30. +hold in high value such men as he is; because on account of Christ's work he was at death's very door,[11] playing+ as it were the +gambler with his life,[12] that he might+ (lit., "may") +supply your lack+, do the service which you could not do, and so complete your loving purposes, in regard +of the ministration+ you designed +for me+.

Our present section illustrates well the inexhaustible variety of Scripture. That pregnant Christian thinker, the late Dr John Ker, has some good sentences on this subject: "What varieties are in the Bible, side by side! The Book of Ruth, with its pastoral quiet after the wars of the Judges, like an innocent child which has crept between the ranks of hostile armies; the intense devotion of the Psalms after the speculative discussions of Job, and before the practical wisdom of Proverbs; the gloom of Ecclesiastes, and then the sweetness of the Song of Solomon, as sharply divided as the eastern morning which leaps from the night, or, as an old Greek might have said, silver-footed Thetis rising from the bed of old Tithonus; Isaiah's majestic sweep of eagle pinion, with Jeremiah's dovelike plaint; the cloudlike obscurities of Ezekiel, to be solved, as one might expect, by piercing light from the sky; and the perplexities of Daniel, to be opened by the movements of the nations."[13]

What a variety lies before us here!

"Into the heaven of heavens we have presumed,
And drawn empyreal air";

while the Apostle has told us (only fourteen verses above) how Christ Jesus, in the glory of the Throne, in the Form of God, cared for us men and for our salvation, and made Himself void, and took the creature-nature, and died; and how He is now on the Throne again in His Incarnation, to receive supreme and universal worship. And then again we came back to earth, yet so as to be led into the deep secrets of the Lord in the inner life of His saints below; "God is working in you, to will and to do, for His good pleasure's sake." And then we have seen this inner life expanding and shewing itself in the holy life without, which shines as a star in the dark, and speaks like a voice from the unseen. And then again we have watched the Apostle's martyr-joy as he thinks of dying for his Philippians, if need be. Close upon all these heights and depths now comes in this totally different passage about Timotheus and Epaphroditus, with its quiet, practical allusions to individual character, and to particular circumstances, and to personal hopes and duties; its words of sympathy and sorrow; the dear friend's agitated state of mind; his recent almost fatal illness; the mercy of his recovery; the pleasurable thought of his restoration to the loving circles at Philippi.

Nothing could be more completely different than this from the grand dogmatic passage traversed a little while before, nor again from the passages to follow in the next chapter, where the believer's inmost secrets of acceptance and of life are in view, and his foresight of glory. We are placed here not in the upper heaven, nor before the judgment-throne, nor in the light of the resurrection-morning. We are just in the "hired rooms" at Rome, and we see the Missionary seated there, studying the characters of two of his brethren, and weighing the reasons for asking them, at once or soon, to arrange for a certain journey. He reviews the case, and then he puts down, through his amanuensis, for the information of the Philippians, what he thinks of these two men, and what he has planned about them.

All is perfectly human, viewed from one side. I or my reader may at any time, in the course of life and duty, be called upon to write about Christian friends and fellow-workers of our own in a tone neither less nor more human and practical than that of this section. In any collection of modern Christian letters we may find the like. I open at this moment the precious volume of Henry Martyn's correspondence, published (1844) as a companion to the Memoir. There I read as follows, in a letter to Daniel Corrie, dated Shiraz, December 12, 1811: "Your accounts of the progress of the kingdom of God among you are truly refreshing. Tell dear H. and the men of both regiments that I salute them much in the Lord, and make mention of them in my prayers. May I continue to hear thus of their state; and if I am spared to see them again, may we make it evident that we have grown in grace. Affectionate remembrances to your sister and to S. I hope they continue to prosecute their labours of love. Remember me to the people of Cawnpore who enquire. Why have I not mentioned Colonel P.? It is not because he is not in my heart, for there is hardly a man in the world whom I love and honour more. My most Christian salutations to him. May the grace of our Lord Jesus Christ be with your spirit, dearest brother. Yours affectionately, H. MARTYN."

What is the difference in quality and character between this extract and our present section of Philippians, or between it and many another passage in the Pauline Epistles? From one point of view, I repeat it, none—none that we either can, or should care to, affirm. Of the letters compared, one is as purely human as the other, in the simplicity of its topics, in its local and personal scope, in its natural and individual manner. I would add that, so far as we can tell, the one was written under just as much or little consciousness of a supernatural prompting as the other. I feel sure that when St Paul wrote thus (whatever might be his sense of an *afflatus* at other times, when he wrote, or spoke, or thought, abnormally) he "felt" exactly as we feel when writing a quiet letter; he was thinking, arranging topics, choosing words, considering the needs of correspondents, just as simply as we might do.

And all this is an element inestimably precious in the structure and texture of the Bible. It is that side or aspect of the Bible which, at least to innumerable minds, brings the whole Book, in a sense so genuine, *home*; making it felt in the human heart as a friend truly conversant with our nature and our life. "Thy testimonies," writes the Bible-loving Psalmist (Ps. cxix. 24), "are the men of my counsel," *an'shêy 'atsâthî*; a pregnant phrase, which puts vividly before us "the human element" of the blessed Word, its varieties and individualities, its *living* voice, or rather voices, and the sympathetic confidence which it invites as it draws close to us to advise and guide. How perfectly in contrast are the Bible on the one side, with this humanity and companionship, and such a "sacred book" as the Koran on the other, with its monotonous oracles! Strange, that the man-made "sacred book" should be so little *humane* and the God-made Book so deeply and beautifully so! Yet not strange, after all. For God knows man better than man knows himself; and when He prepares a Book of books for man, we may expect it to correspond to the deep insight of Him who is Maker of both the volume and the reader.

For now on the other part we have to remember that this Book, so naturally and humanly written, as to a very large proportion of its contents, is yet God-made all through. It is, in a sense quite peculiar to itself, divine. I quoted a passage from a letter of Henry Martyn's just now, on purpose to place it beside this letter of St Paul's, with a view to shewing the likeness of the two. But are they like in all respects? No; they present a radical difference from another side. It is just this, that the biblical letter is not only human as to its type and utterance; as to its message, it is authoritative, it is from God. Henry Martyn writes as a Christian man, and it helps us spiritually to be in contact with his affectionate and holy thoughts. Paul writes as a Christian man, but also as "a chosen vessel to bear the Name" of his Lord; as the messenger of the mind of Christ; as he who received "his Gospel" "not of man, nor by man, but by the revelation of Jesus Christ" (Gal. i. 12). From his own days to these he has been known in the Church of God as the divinely commissioned prophet and teacher. Clement of Rome in the first century refers to him as having written to Corinth by divine inspiration.[14] Simon Peter, earlier than Clement, refers to Paul (2 Pet. iii. 16) as the writer of "Scriptures," *graphai*: that solemn word, restricted in the language of Christianity to the oracles of God.

The simplest and seemingly most naturalistic passage occurring in a Pauline letter is a "Scripture"; and as such it speaks to me only not like the utterances of a Martyn but with the voice of the Lord of the Gospel. "Paul, Paul—his letters I have read, but not always I agree with him!" So, according to the story, said a German literary visitor in an Oxford common-room, fifty years ago; the words shocked the Anglican company. Very many people think with the German now, whether or no they have really "*read* Paul's letters." But their thought is not that of the Church of God; and the soul that will indeed make experiment of what "Paul's letters" can be when they are read as divine, and before God, will surely find itself in harmony in this matter with the Church. It will be little disposed to take up the cry (true enough in itself), "Back to Christ," in that false sense which discredits the servant's words as if the Master was not committed to them. "If they have kept My saying, they will keep yours also."

In a passage like the present therefore we feel the two elements or aspects, the human and the divine, each real and powerful, and both working in perfect harmony. The human is there, not in the least as a necessary element of error; rather as an element of delicate and beautiful truth, the truth of justest thought and feeling. The divine is there, as the message from Christ Himself through His servant; sacred, authoritative, binding on belief, giving solid ground for the soul's repose. We study here St Paul's watchful and unselfish remembrance of the Philippians, in the case of Timothy and his mission, and still more in that of Epaphroditus. We recognize of course the actings of a noble human heart, and we are right to do so. But we find more than this; we see JESUS CHRIST informing us, in the concrete example of His servant, exactly how it behoves us, as His servants, to feel and act under our responsibilities. St Paul's thought and action is "written for our learning." True, the "learning" comes not as a mere code, or lecture. It takes the form of a living experience, recorded, in the course of correspondence, by the man who is going through it. But the man is a vehicle of revelation. He writes about himself; but his Master is behind him, and is taking care that his whole thought shall be the well-adjusted conveyance of a thought greater than his own.

As we come to the incidental details of the passage, we find the same double aspect of Scripture everywhere. St Paul speaks about people who are "seeking their own interests, and not the interests of Jesus Christ" (ver. 21). He says this quite naturally, and with a reference quite local and in detail. But on the other side the words are an oracle; they convey the message of the Master of His people; they implicitly claim *on His part* that we shall seek not our own interests, but His. Again, quite in passing, the Apostle speaks of this or that "hope" or "trust" as being formed "in the Lord." He does so with no conscious dogmatic purpose, surely; it is because it comes as naturally to him to do it as for an ordinary correspondent to say that he hopes to do this or that "if all goes well." But in the epistolary *Scripture* these brief phrases have another side; they are authority and oracle; they convey the mind of Christ about *our* right relations with Him; they tell *us*, from Him, that it is His will that we too, as His, should form our hopes and plans "in Him," in conscious recollection of our being His members.

St Paul speaks again of his human sensibilities. He tells us of his sorrows, and his longings for encouragement, and his thankfulness that an aggravation of trial, "sorrow upon sorrow," has been spared him. He speaks of Epaphroditus, and of his generous carelessness of his own health and life, and of the illness he had contracted, and of his merciful recovery, and of his home-sick longing for Philippi, and of his "bewilderment" of regret as he thinks of the Philippians' anxiety about him. All this is quite as naturally and "humanly" conceived and written on St Paul's part as anything that I or my reader ever wrote about joys and griefs, our own or of our friends. But not one whit the less is this all a message, an oracle, from our Lord Jesus Christ, in a sense in which no letter of ours could possibly be such. For it is a "Scripture." And so it tells me *from above* that the free and loving exercise of human sympathies is entirely according to the will of God; that human tears and longings are in perfect harmony with holiness. It assures me that from one point of view it is right to speak of the prolongation of the believer's life as a "mercy," even though "to depart is to be with Christ, which is far better." It assures me, let me notice by the way, that bodily sickness is not by any means necessarily a direct result or index of sinfulness in the sufferer. There are those who think and say that it is. But this is not the view of the "chosen vessel." He sees no sin in Epaphroditus' "falling ill, nigh unto death," "drawing near, up to death." It is for him only an occasion for fresh gratitude and affection towards the sufferer, and for deep thanksgivings to Him who in His mercy has granted the recovery. All this is not only an experience, recorded with beautiful naturalness; it is a revelation, an oracle. We learn by it, as by the voice of Christ, that although "He took our infirmities and bare our sicknesses," His servants do not therefore of necessity fail in either faith or love when they suffer "in this tabernacle," and "groan, being burthened." Let them look indeed with great simplicity, in humble faith, for the healing power of their Lord, whether or not it may please Him to apply it through human agency. But do not let them think it an act of faith to dictate to Him, as it were, the necessity of their physical recovery. "If it be Thy will," is never out of place in such appeals. Faith can breathe its most absolute and restful reliance into that "If."

We close the section of Timotheus and Epaphroditus. We have given our main thought to the light which it throws upon the nature of the Scriptures, those blessed "men of our counsel." We have scarcely turned aside to think of the actual "men" of the passage; Timotheus, and his self-forgetting devotion to the Lord and to St Paul, overcoming the sensitiveness of a tender nature; Epaphroditus, at once brave and affectionate, yearning for the old friends in the old scene, restless in the thought of their trouble about him, yet ready to "throw his life down as a die" in the cause of God and of His people. But if we have said little about them, it is not that we do not love their very names, and feel our union with them.

"Once they were mourning here below";

finding then, as we find now, that the day's burthen is no dream. But we shall see them hereafter, in the mercy of God, "changed and glorified," yet the same, where there will be leisure to learn all the lessons that all the saints can teach us from their experience of the love of Jesus.

Meanwhile let us pray, with the Moravians in their beautiful Liturgy:

*Keep us in everlasting fellowship with our brethren of the Church triumphant, and let us rest together in Thy presence from our labours.*

[1] *Timotheon* is slightly emphatic by its place in the Greek; as if to say, "Though *I* must still be absent, *he* will soon be with you."

[2] Not "equal-souled *with myself*"; which would demand rather, in the Greek, *oudena allon echô isopsychon.*

[3] Possibly, "*entered on* bondservice," "*took up* the slave's life," with a reference to Timothy's earliest connexion with St Paul (Acts xvi. 1-3). But the reference to the memories of *Philippi* is much more likely. The aorist, *edouleusen*, will in this case gather up into one the whole recollection.

[4] The *touton* is slightly emphatic by position, for St Paul is about to speak of other persons also, himself and Epaphroditus.

[5] *Êgêsamên*: I render the epistolary past by a present tense, which is the English idiom.

[6] So I render *apostolon*, to represent something of the *sacredness* attaching by usage to the word. If I read aright, we have here an instance of gentle pleasantry, quite in harmony with the gravity of the Epistle at large. He takes the Philippians' message of love and gift of bounty as a sort of *gospel* to himself, and so regards their messenger as a *missionary* to him. So also with the word *leitourgos*: its usual associations in New Testament Greek are sacred, or at least solemn; and so St Paul seems to employ it here. Epaphroditus was no mere agent; he was a "*ministrant*," commissioned from a high quarter—the Philippians' love.

[7] *epeidê epidothôn ên*: the epistolary past (*ên*) is rendered in accordance with English idiom. *Epipothôn* is perhaps too *heavily* rendered above; but the phrase is certainly a little stronger than *epepothei* would have been.

[8] Perhaps it was an attack of Roman fever.

[9] *Ina mê … schô*: lit., "that I *may* not." But the English idiom asks for "might." The Greek puts the past intention into what *was* its present aspect.

67

[10] *Epempsa auton*: the epistolary aorist.

[11] Quite literally, "up to death he drew near." It is as if St Paul had been about to write, *mechri thanatou êsthense*, and then varied the expression by writing *êggise*.

[12] *Paraboleusamenos tê psychê*: so read, not *paraboleusamenos* (which would mean, "taking evil counsel for his life," neglecting its interests). *Paraboleusamenos* is a well-attested reading; the verb is not found elsewhere, but the form is abundantly likely. It would be developed from the adjective *parabolos*, "reckless," connected with the verb *paraballesthai*, "to cast a die."

[13] *Thoughts for Heart and Life*, by John Ker, D.D. (1888), p. 92.

[14] See Ep. i. *ad. Cor.*, § 47: "Take up the Epistle of the blessed Paul, the Apostle… . He wrote to you in the Spirit (*pneumatikôs*) about himself, and Cephas, and Apollos."

"One family we dwell in Him,
One Church, above, beneath,
Though now divided by the stream,
The narrow stream of death.

"One army of the living God
To His command we bow;
Part of His host hath cross'd the flood,
And part is crossing now."
C. WESLEY.

# *JOY IN THE LORD AND ITS PRESERVING POWER: "THAT I MAY KNOW HIM"*

O Almighty God, whom truly to know is everlasting life; Grant us perfectly to know Thy Son Jesus Christ to be the way, the truth, and the life; that, following the steps of Thy holy Apostles, we may stedfastly walk in the way that leadeth to eternal life; through the same Thy Son Jesus Christ our Lord. Amen.

Collect for St Philip and St James.

## CHAPTER VIII

### JOY IN THE LORD AND ITS PRESERVING POWER "THAT I MAY KNOW HIM"

PHILIPPIANS iii. 1-11

Doctrinal perils at Philippi—"Be glad in the Lord"—The true Israel—An ideal legalist—Position and experience—The spiritual power of holy joy— Acceptance and holiness—Atoning Cross and Risen Life

With the section just closed the Epistle reaches its middle point and already looks towards its end. We may lawfully think of St Paul as pausing here in his dictation; he returns to it after some considerable interval, with new topics, or rather with one important new topic, in his mind. Hitherto, if we have read him aright, we have seen him occupied, from one side or another, with the thought of Christian Unity at Philippi. That thought has been either explicitly developed, as in the close of the first chapter, and in the opening of the second, and again in the passage embracing ii. 14-16; or it has been rather implied than expounded. The Apostle's assurances of love and prayer have been often worded so as to suggest it. The grand passage of doctrine, ii. 5-11, has been occasioned directly by it, and is made to bear immediately upon it; the Lord's wonderful self-abnegation (if the word may be tolerated) is revealed and asserted there, not in an isolated way, but as it speaks to the believer of the spirit which should animate *him*, and which will preclude jealousies and separations as nothing else can. And even the paragraph where Timotheus and Epaphroditus are before us is tinged with the same feeling; what the Apostle says about both these dear friends is so said as *to unite* the sympathies of the Philippians.

But he has more to speak of than this sacred call to union of spirit and of life in Christ. We gather that Epaphroditus, talking over the condition of the Mission with his leader, had alluded to the presence there of serious doctrinal perils, which must ultimately affect Christian holiness. That ubiquitous difficulty, the propaganda of anti-Pauline Christian Judaism, had come on the scene, or was just coming. The teachers who affirmed, or insinuated, that Jesus Christ could be reached only through the ceremonial law, were now to be reckoned with. The converts were disturbed, or soon might be disturbed, by being told that proselytism to Moses, sealed by circumcision, was a *sine quâ non* in order to a valid hope of salvation through the Gospel; that the man awakened from his paganism must be at least something of a Jew to be anything of a Christian; that the door was *not* absolutely open between the sinner's soul and the Saviour, to be passed through by the one step of a living trust in the Promise.

Let us remember that assertions like these, which to Christians now may seem obviously futile, by no means necessarily seemed so then. Then, much more than now, pagan enquirers after JESUS would be sure to be conscious that the true salvation offered was, in one sense, emphatically a Jewish salvation. It was the message which told of the life and death, the person and work, of One who *was*, "after the flesh," a Jew. It was the announcement that the long hope of *Israel* was fulfilled in Him. Its terminology was full of words and ideas altogether Jewish. And its messengers—above all, for the Philippians, St Paul —were Jews, of unmistakable nationality, training, and (doubtless) appearance. On a first view, on a hasty and shallow view certainly, it may have seemed a quite natural incident in such a message when some of its propagandists asserted that to reach this Hebrew Deliverer and King the enquirer must form a connexion in religion which should be definitely Hebrew.

It is conceivable that even yet, in the history of the Church, this phase of error may in some form assert itself again. We look in the future, it may be in the near future, for the keeping to the old Israel of promises which have never been revoked. We believe that Rom. xi. shall yet find its fulfilment, and that the "receiving of them again shall be life from the dead" to the world. In that great period of blessing, the work of missions may (shall we not say, probably will?) be very largely taken up by Hebrew Christians. And if any of these, like some of their predecessors of the first age, should have only a distorted view of the Gospel of Christ, their intense national character may tell not a little on the form of their message. But this is by the way. All that is really before us here is the fact that—not the open hostility of unconverted Jews but —the sidelong counter-action of Judaistic Christians was threatening Philippi, and must be met by the Apostle.

Nor was this, if we explain rightly the close of ch. iii., the only such danger in the air. The antinomian traitor was also within the gates. There were those who could assert that the Gospel, the Pauline Gospel, the wonderful message of Justification by Faith only, and of a life lived in the Spirit as its sequel, was the very truth they held and rejoiced in; but they taught it so as to reason from it that practical holiness did not matter; the justified, the accepted, the man of the Spirit, lived in a transcendental religious region; he was not to be bound in conduct by common rules. Was he not in grace? And was not grace the antithesis of works? Was not grace, before everything else, the condonation of sin? And the more it did that work, was it not the more glorious? "Shall we not continue in sin then, that grace may abound?" What does it signify, though the perishable and burthensome body defiles itself? The emancipated spirit of the "spiritual" man lives on another plane; the sensual and the mystical elements may approach, may run parallel, but can never meet. The body may sin; the spirit must be pure—if only the man is in grace.

Such assuredly were some of the conditions of error and evil to be considered when on that far-off day, in his Roman chamber, St Paul turned his soul again to Philippi, and asked his scribe to write. There is a solemn comfort in the thought. In our days of trial, when again and again it is as it "the foundations were destroyed," it is something to remember the awful mental and moral trials of the apostolic age. It was indeed an "age of faith"; but, as the other side of that very fact, it was an age of clouds and darkness, from the point not of "faith" but of "sight." It had a glorious answer to the tremendous questions that beset it. But that answer was not human reasoning, or material successes; it was the Lord Jesus Christ. And so it is for us to-day.

But now St Paul is at work; let us listen, and we shall hear how promptly he brings that answer to bear in his letter to Philippi.[1]

Ver. 1. For the rest (*to loipon*), my brethren, to turn now to another topic, as I draw towards an end, let me give you this comprehensive watchword +Be glad in the Lord+.[2] +To write the same things to you+, to reiterate that one thought, that CHRIST is our glory and our joy, "+to me not irksome, it is safe for you+."[3] Safe, because there are spiritual dangers around you from which this will be the best preservative; false teachings which can only be fully met with the gladness of the truth of Christ. +Beware of+,

Ver. 2. keep your eyes open upon (*blepete*), +the "dogs,"+ the men who would *excommunicate* all who hold not with their half-Christian Pharisaism and its legal burthens, but who are themselves thus self-excluded from the covenant blessing. +Beware of the evil workmen+, the teachers whose watchword is "works, works, works," a weary round of observances and would-be merits, but who are sorry *work-men* indeed, spoiling the whole structure of "Heaven's easy, artless, unencumber'd plan." +Beware of the concision+, the apostles of a mere physical wounding, which, as enjoined according to their principles, is nothing better than a mutilation (*katatomê*), a parody of what circumcision was meant to be, as the sacrament of a preparatory dispensation now terminated in its

Ver. 3. fulfilment. +For+ not they but +we are the circumcision+, the true Israel of the true covenant, sealed and purified by our God; +we who by God's Spirit worship+,[4] doing priestly service in a spiritual temple[5] in a life, love, and power, which is ours by the presence in us of the Holy Ghost, the promise of the Father; +and who exult+, not in tribal, national, ceremonial prerogatives, but +in Christ Jesus+, our refuge and our crown, our righteousness and glory, with an exultation infinitely warmer than the legalist's can be, and meanwhile pure, for its source is altogether not ourselves; +and who+, in Him, +not in the flesh+,[6] not in self and its workings, +are confident+ (for confident we are, but it is a "confidence in self-despair," the confidence of those who have been driven by self-discovery to Christ alone).[7] I speak with a general reference, of all true disciples; but let me instance myself as a case peculiarly in point. I speak thus,

Ver. 4. +though having+ (*echôn*), I, myself (*egô*), from *their* view-point, +confidence even in flesh+. +Whoever else thinks of confiding in flesh+, of building a legal standing-place on his privilege and merit, +I+ may do so +more+ than he; for I have reached the *ne plus ultra* in that

Ver. 5. direction. +As for circumcision+,[8] I was an +eight-day+ child; no proselyte, operated upon in later life, but a son of the Covenant; descended +from Israel's race+, one of the progeny of him who was a prince with God (Gen. xxxii. 28); +of Benjamin's tribe+, the tribe which gave the first God-chosen king to the nation, and which remained "faithful among the faithless" to the house of David at a later day; +Hebrew+ offspring +of Hebrew ancestors+,[9] child of a home in which, immemorially, the old manners and the old speech were cherished; *in respect of the law,[10] a Pharisee*—the votary of religious precision, elaborate devotion, exclusive privilege, and energetic prose-

Ver. 6, lytism; +in respect of zeal+, intense and perfectly sincere, +persecuting the Church+; in respect of the righteousness which+ resides +in the Law+, as its terms are understood by the Pharisee, +found+ (*genomenos*) +blameless+.[11] Such was my position. I possessed an ideal pedigree; full sacramental position from the first; domestic traditions pure and strict; an absolute personal devotion to the cause of my creed; the most rigorous observance of its rules; the most energetic

Ver. 7. efforts to maintain and extend its power. +But the kind of things which+ (*hatina*) +I felt+ (*moi ên*) so many *gains,[12] these things I have come to consider* (*hegemai*, perfect), +because of our+ (*ton*) +Christ+ (discovered at last in His glory, as the slain and risen Jesus), just one +loss+, one +deprivation+; not merely a worthless thing, but a ruinous one; a robbery of the true Blessing

Ver. 8. from my soul. +Aye more, I actually+ (*kai*) now +consider all things+, from all points of view, all possessions, all ambitions, +to be+ similarly +loss+, deprivation, +because of the surpassingness of the knowledge of Christ Jesus my Lord+, because of the immeasurable betterness of a spirit-sight of what HE is, in Himself, and as my own; +because of whom+—on account of what He now was to me—+I suffered deprivation+ (*exêmiôthên*) +of my all+ (*ta panta*), in the crisis of my change; +and I consider it+ only +refuse+,[13] rubbish, that +I may gain+[14] (in a blessed exchange of profit against loss, the loss of what I thought my "gains") +Christ+, nothing less than HIM, my boundless Wealth (*ploutos*

Ver. 9. *anexichniaston*, Eph. iii. 8), +and be found+, at any and every "time of finding" (Ps. xxxii. 7, Heb.) by the Holy One, +in Him+, one with Him, in His precious merits and in His risen life, but now especially in His merits; +not having a righteousness of my own, that derived from the Law+, a title to acceptance drawn from my own supposed perfect correspondence to the Law, +but that which+ comes +through faith in[15] Christ+, through reliance wholly reposed in Him, +the righteousness which is derived+ not from the Law but +from God+, coming wholly out of His uncaused and sacred mercy, +on terms of our (*tê*) faith+, conditioned[15]

Ver. 10. to us by simply our accepting reliance; +in order to know Him+, HIM, my Lord, with an intuition possible only to the soul which accepts Him for its All; +and the power of His Resurrection+, as that Resurrection assures His people of their justification (Rom. iv. 24, 25), and of their coming glory (1 Cor. xv. 20), and yet more as He, by His life-giving Spirit, shed forth from Him the risen Head, lives His "indissoluble life" (Heb. vii. 16) in His members; and +the partnership of His sufferings+, that deep experience of union with Him which comes through daily "taking up the cross," in His steps, for His sake, and in His strength; growing into conformity (*summorthi-xomenos*, a present participle) +with His Death+, drawn evermore into spiritual harmony with Him who wrought my salvation out by an ineffable surrender

Ver. 11. of Himself to suffer; if +somehow I may arrive+, along the appointed path of the believer's obedience, +at the resurrection which is out from the dead+ (*tên exanastasin tên ex nekrôn*: so read); "that blessed hope" for all who sleep in Him, when their whole existence, redeemed and perfected, shall leave the world of "the dead" behind for ever.

Here is a piece of consecutive rendering and paraphrase longer than usual. And meanwhile the passage before us is one of extraordinary fulness and richness, alike in its record of experience and its teaching of eternal truths. But it seemed impossible to break into fragments the glorious wholeness of the Apostle's thought and utterance. And then, the utterance is so rich, so detailed, so explanatory of itself, that I could not but feel that, for very much of it at least, my best commentary was the closest rendering I could offer, with a few brief suggestions by the way.

Drawing now to a close, I can only indicate, under one or two headings, some main messages to the mind and soul.

i. I gather from the connexion of the passage, as we have traced it, the supreme importance of a true joy in the Lord, a true personal sight of "the King in His beauty," in order to our spiritual orthodoxy. Let me quote again from the Prayer Book of the Moravians, from which I gave one short extract in the last chapter. In their "Church Litany," among the first suffrages, occur these petitions: *From coldness to Thy merits and death. From error and misunderstanding, From the loss of our glory in Thee, Preserve us, gracious Lord and God.*" The words are the very soul of St Paul, as it conveys the Spirit's oracle to us here. St Paul dreads exceedingly for the Philippians the incursion of "error and misunderstanding"; the advent of a mechanical rigorism of rule and ordinance, and (as we shall see in later pages) the subtle poison also of the specious antinomian lie. How does he apply the antidote? In the form of an appeal to them to be sure to not to "lose their glory in the Lord"; and then he writes a record of his own experience in which he shews them how his own Pharisaic treasures had all been cast away, or willingly given up to the spoiler; and why? Not for abstract reasons, but "because of the surpassingness of the knowledge of Christ Jesus my Lord"; because of the irresistible and infinite *betterness* of His discovered glory, seen in the atoning Cross and the Resurrection power.

Let us "arm ourselves likewise with the same mind." We have countless perils about us in our modern Christendom, things which only too easily can trouble the reason and sway the will away from the one "hope set before us." Let us meet them, whatever else we do, with the Moravians' prayer. Let us meet them with obedience to the Apostle's positive injunction, "Rejoice in the Lord."

ii. The passage bids us remember the profound connexion between a true "knowledge" of the Lord Jesus as our Atonement and a true "knowledge" of Him as our Life and Power. Both are here. In ver. 9, so it seems to me, any unprejudiced reader of St Paul's writings must see language akin to those great passages of Romans and Galatians which put before us the supreme question of our Justification, and which send us for our whole hope of Acceptance before the eternal Judge, whose law we have broken, to the Atoning Death of our Lord Jesus Christ. In those passages, demonstrably as I venture to think, the word "Righteousness" is largely used as a short term for the Holy One's righteous way of accepting us sinners for the sake of the Sinless One, who, in our nature, was "made a curse for us," "made sin for us," "delivered for our offences," "set forth for a propitiation," that we might be "justified from all things" in our union with Him by faith. If so, this is the purport of similar phrases here also. St Paul is thinking here first of the discovered glory of Christ as the propitiation for his sins, his peace with God, his refuge and his rest for ever against the accuser and the curse. That comes first, profoundly first.

But then we have also here the sequel truth, the glorious complement. Here is Acceptance, wholly for Jesus Christ's most blessed sake. But this is but the divine condition to another divine and transcendent blessing; it is revealed as the way in to a knowledge of this Lord of Peace, a deep and unspeakable knowledge of Him, such as shall infuse into His disciple the power of His Risen Life, and the secret of an inward assimilation of the soul to the very principle of His Death, and shall be the path whose end shall be His glory.

St Paul here bids us never put asunder what God hath joined together. "Never further than the Cross, never higher than Thy feet"; there may we be "found," "in Him"; unshaken by surrounding mysteries, and meekly resolute against fashions of opinion. Let us be recognized for those who truly know for themselves, and truly commend to others, that blessed "Justification by Faith" which is still, as ever, the Beautiful Gate of the Gospel.

> "'Tis joy enough, my All in All,
>   Before Thy feet to lie;
> Thou wilt not let me lower fall,
>   And who can higher fly?"

But then let us be known as those who, accepting Christ Jesus as our All for peace, (whatever we may have to "consider to be loss" that we may do so,) have clasped Him also as our Hidden Life, our Risen Power, our King within.

> "O Jesus Christ, grow Thou in me,
>   And all things else recede;
> My heart be daily nearer Thee,
>   From sin be daily freed." [17]

Always at the atoning Cross;—yes, every day and hour; "knowing no other stand" before the face of the Holy One. Always receiving there the Risen

Life, the presence inwardly of the Risen One, the secret power to suffer and to serve in peace;—yes, for ever yes; "to the praise of the glory of His grace."

So, and only so, shall we live the life of real sinners really saved; "worshipping by the Spirit of God, exulting in Christ Jesus, and confident, but not in the flesh."

[1] The reader may be aware that Bishop Lightfoot's theory of the connexion of thought at the beginning of ch. iii. is different from that advocated here. He thinks that St Paul dictated on continuously *till the close of* iii. 1, and was interrupted there, and then began *de novo* with iii. 2, entirely on another line. In this view, the words about "writing *the same things* unto you" refer still to *Christian unity*, on which St Paul was going to dilate further, but a sudden pause occurred, and the theme was dropped. With reverence for the great expositor, I cannot but think this unlikely. It assumes that St Paul was curiously indifferent to the sequence of thought in an important apostolic message, which assuredly he would *read over again* before it was actually sent. A theory which fairly explains the passage, and meanwhile avoids the thought of such indifference, seems to me far preferable.

[2] The words obviously may be rendered, "*Farewell* in the Lord"; and so some take them, explaining that St Paul was intending to close immediately, and so wrote his "Adieu" here; but then changed his plan. This is very unlikely however. See below, iv. 4: *Chairete en Kuriô pantote*. The "always" there scarcely suits a formula *of farewell*, while it perfectly suits an injunction *to be glad*. And that passage is the obvious echo of this.—A.V. and R.V. both render "rejoice," though R.V. writes "or, *farewell*" in the margin. St Chrysostom in his comments here explains the passage as referring to the Christian's joy (*chara*). The ancient Latin versions render *Gaudete* (not *valete*) in *Domino*.

[3] I thus render *rhythmically* the rhythmical Greek (it is an iambic trimeter): *emoi men ouk oknêron, humin d asphales*. It is probable that the words are a quotation from a Greek poet, perhaps a "comic" poet; the "comedies" being full of neatly expressed reflexions. For such a quotation, probably from the "comedian" Menander, see 1 Cor. xv. 33: *phtheirousin êthê chrêsth homiliai kakai*: "*Ill converse cankers fair morality.*"

[4] The reading *pneumati Theou* (not *Theô*) *latreuontes* is to be preferred.

[5] *Datreuien* means first to do servants' work, then to do religious "service" (so almost always in LXX. and N.T.) and sometimes specially *priestly* duty (see e.g. Heb. xiii. 10). This latter may be in view here: we Christians, born anew of the Spirit, are the true *priests*, and we little need to be made Jewish proselytes first.

[6] The *sarx* in St Paul is very fairly represented by the word "self" as used popularly in religious language. It is man taken as apart from God, and so man *versus* God; then by transition it may mean, as here, the products of such a source, the labours of the self-life to construct a self-righteousness. It is hardly necessary to say that, in such contexts as this, where it stands more or less distinguished from the *pneuma*, it is not a synonym for "the body." Sins of "the flesh" may be sins purely of the mind, as e.g. "emulation" (Gal. v. 20).

[7] I thus attempt to convey the emphasis of the words *ouk en sarki pepoithotes*, which is not precisely as if he had written *en sarki*.

[8] *Peritouê*: a dative of reference, a frequent construction with St Paul. See Rom. xii. 10-12 for several examples together.

[9] See Trench, *Synonyms*, § xxxix., for the special meanings of *Israêlitês*, the member of the Covenant-people; *Ebraios*, the Jew who was true to his inmost national traditions; and *Ioudaios*, the Jew merely as other than the Gentile.

[10] The article is absent; but context leaves no doubt of the special reference here.

[11] In solemn contrast but with perfect consistency, from another point of view—that not of the Pharisee but of GOD—he can point out elsewhere that "no flesh" can possibly claim "righteousness" on the ground of fulfilment of code and precept. See especially Rom. iii. 19, 20. But his business here is to meet the legalist on the legalist's own ground.

[12] Notice the *plural*; as if, miser-like, he had counted his bags of treasure. And then see the contrasted *singular*, *Xêmian*: he finds them all *one mass of loss*.

[13] *Skubala*: the Greek etymologists derived the word from *kusi balein*, "to cast to dogs." Otherwise it is traced to a connexion with *skôr*, "excrement."

[14] Practically, he means "that I *might* gain," in the past transaction of conversion and surrender. He thinks the past over again.

[15] Lit., "faith of," *pisteôs Christou*. This use of the genitive with *pistis*, to denote its object, is frequent. Cp. e.g. Mark xi. 22; Gal. ii. 16, 20.

[16] Even as the benefit of food is conditioned to us by our (not buying but) eating it.

[17] See the whole hymn (rendered from Lavater's *O Jesu Christe, wachs in mir*) in *Hymns of Consecration*, 295.

"We will dwell on Calvary's mountain
 Where the flocks of Zion feed,
  Oft resorting to that fountain

Open'd when our Lord did bleed;
 Thence deriving
Grace, and life, and holiness."
 *From the Moravian Hymn-book.*

# CHRISTIAN STANDING AND CHRISTIAN PROGRESS

"I want that adorning divine
　Thou only, my God, can'st bestow;
I want in those beautiful garments to shine
　Which distinguish Thy household below.

"I want, as a traveller, to haste
　Straight onward, nor pause on my way,
Nor forethought nor anxious contrivance to waste
　On the tent only pitch'd for a day.

"I want—and this sums up my prayer—
　To glorify Thee till I die,
Then calmly to yield up my soul to Thy care,
　And breathe out, in faith, my last sigh."
　　　CHARLOTTE ELLIOTT.

# CHAPTER IX

### CHRISTIAN STANDING AND CHRISTIAN PROGRESS

PHILIPPIANS iii. 12-16

Christian exultation—Christian confidence—"Not in the flesh"—"In Jesus Christ"—The prize in view—No finality in the progress—"Not already perfect"—The recompense of reward—What the prize will be

In a certain sense we have completed our study of the first section of the third chapter of the Epistle. But the treatment has been so extremely imperfect, in view of the importance of that section, that a few further remarks must be made. Let us ponder one weighty verse, left almost unnoticed when we touched it.

Observe then the brief, pregnant *account of the true Christian*, given in ver. 3: "We are the circumcision, we who by God's Spirit worship, and who exult in Christ Jesus, and who, not in the flesh, are confident." This is a far-reaching description of the true member of the true Israel, the man of the Covenant of grace.

Note first its positive lines. *"We worship," "we exult," "we are confident."* Every affirmation is full of divine principles of truth. *"We worship"*; ours is a hallowed, dedicated, and reverent life. It is spent in a sanctuary. Whatever we have to be, or to do, as to externals; whether to rule a province, a church, a school, a home; whether to keep accounts, or sweep a room; whether to evangelize the slums of a city, or the dark places of heathenism, or to teach language, or science, or music; whether to be active all day long, or to lie down alone to suffer; whatever be our actual place and duty in the world, *"we worship."* "We have set the Lord always before us." We have "sanctified Christ as LORD in our hearts" (1 Pet. iii. 15; so read). We belong to Him everywhere, and we recollect it. We owe adoring reverence to Him everywhere, and we recollect it. Let us reiterate the fact; ours is a hallowed life, for it belongs to a divine Master; it is a reverent life, for that Master in His greatness is to us an abiding Presence. The fact of Him, the thought of Him, has expelled from our lives the secular air and the light and flippant spirit. We are nothing if not *worshippers*.

Then, secondly, *"we exult."* Ours is a life of gladness, so far as it is the true Christian life. Constantly and profoundly chastened by its worshipping character, it is constantly quickened and illuminated by this element of exultation. The word is strong, *kauchômenoi*, "exulting." We observe that the

Apostle does not say that we are resigned, that we are at peace, that there is a calm upon us. This is true; but he says that "we *exult*." The "still waters," the *mêy m'nûchôth* of Ps. xxiii. 2, are anything but stagnant. They are a lake; but it is a lake upon a river, like the fair waters of Galilee, receiving and giving, and therefore alive with pure movement, while yet surrounded by the "rest," *m'nûchâh*, which means repose not *from* action but *underneath* it. "We exult." Ours is not an autumn of feeling; not a state of the soul in which the characteristics are the sighs and starting tears of memory and apprehension. It is an everlasting spring, in which the mighty but temperate Sun of Salvation is shining, and will not set; not parching but quickening all day long. "We exult." It is a happy life, not only with the happiness of a cheerful contentment, beautiful as that is; ours is the happiness of wondering discovery, and rich possession, and ever-opening prospects; it is "quick and lively"; it is "exultation."

Then, "*we are confident*." If I traced the bearing of this clause aright, in the last chapter, we shall feel that the word *pepoithotes* is meant to carry a *positive* message. It is not only that "we do not rely on the flesh"; it is that "we are reliant, though not on the flesh." Even so, in the true idea of the Christian life. "*We are confident*." We are not wanderers from one peradventure to another; we are reliant, we are assured, we know where we are, and what we are, and whither we are bound. True, we, are intensely conscious of the limits of our knowledge; it is only here and there that we can absolutely say, "We know." But then, the points where we *can* say so are points of supreme importance. "We know that the Son of God is come." "We know that our sins are forgiven us for His name's sake." "We know that all things work together for good to them that love God." "We know that if our earthly house of this tabernacle is dissolved, we have a building of God, a house not made with hands, eternal in the heavens; therefore we are always *confident*." And all this is summed up in the thought that "we know WHOM we have believed, and that HE is able to keep what we have committed unto Him." Our certainty is a confiding certainty. It does not reside in our courage, or our mental insight; it is lodged in a Person, who is such that He claims our entire reliance on His work, His word, Himself.

Then from its other side this wonderful verse gives us the cautions, the negatives, of the Christian life; though even here it speaks the language of the highest positive truth. "We worship *by God's Spirit*"; our reverence, our adoration, the hallowing and religiousness of our lives, is not a form imposed from without; it is a power exerting itself from within, having come to our poor hearts from above. Assuredly we do not neglect or slight actions and rites of worship; He who has made each of us soul and body, one man, does not mean us to despise the outward and physical in devotion. But we watchfully remember that no such actions or rites are, for one moment, the soul of worship, or its formative power. *That* soul and power is "God's Spirit" only; the Holy Ghost dwelling in the renewed being, and teaching the man "to cry Abba, Father," and "making intercession for him with groanings which cannot be uttered," and "taking of the things of Christ, and shewing it unto us." We pray, and it is "in the Holy Ghost." We worship, and it is "in Spirit, and in truth."

Again, "we exult *in Christ Jesus*." Our glad and animated happiness lies in nothing short of HIM as its cause. We are thankful for noble religious traditions and institutions, and for holy parentage, and for all which makes Christianity correspond in practice to its name. But we are watchful not to let even these blessings take the unique place of "Christ Jesus" in our "exultation." "In all things He must have the pre-eminence." Piety itself without Him, if it can be found, is not a body but a statue. All the privileges of the Church of God, without Him, though we reverently cherish every teaching and every ordinance that is Christian indeed, are but the frame without the picture, the casket without the stone.

Then again, "*not in the flesh* are we confident." We have learnt a deep distrust of everything which St Paul classes under that word "flesh." It is always offering itself to us, in one Protean shape or another, to be our comfort and our repose. Sometimes it takes the form of our supposed usefulness and diligence; sometimes of our strict and exemplary observances; sometimes, putting on a disguise still more subtle, it sets before the Christian the depth, or the length, of his spiritual experience. Or it grows bolder, and is content with coarser masks; it tempts us to a miserable reliance on some imagined betterness when we compare ourselves, forsooth, with some one else. I knew long ago an old shepherd, in my father's parish, who based a hope for eternity on the fact (if such it was) that he was never tipsy on a Sunday. We are amused, or we are shocked. But this was only an extreme type of a vast phenomenon, to be found lurking in countless hearts, when God lets in the light; the "reliance" on our being somehow, so we think, "not as other men are." And from this whole world of delusion, in all its continents and islands, the Lord calls us away here by His Apostle. He bids us migrate as it were to another planet, laying our *whole* confidence, not part of it, on HIM; let that other world, our old world, roll along without us.

Christ presents to us Himself (as we follow out this rich Philippian passage) as *all* our Righteousness, in His precious justifying Merit, offered for the acceptance of the very simplest faith. And He presents Himself as *all* our Power, for deliverance and for service, in His resurrection Life; coming to reveal Himself to us in the divine beauty of His sufferings, His death, through which he has passed for us into "indissoluble life" (Heb. vii. 16). Our Righteousness—it is HE, "the propitiation for our sins." Our Sanctification—it is still HE, in "the power of His resurrection, and fellowship with His sufferings, and assimilation to His death." Our Redemption, from the power of the grave—it is still "this same Jesus," in union with whom alone we "attain unto the resurrection which is out from the dead."

Even so, Lord Jesus Christ; let us thus be "found in Thee"; worshipping, exulting, confiding; resting on Thee, abiding in Thee, with an accepting faith which only grows more simple and single as the years move on and gather "since we believed."

"Help us, O Christ, to grasp each truth
   With hand as firm and true
As when we clasp'd it first to heart
   A treasure fresh and new;

"To name Thy name, Thyself to own,
   With voice unfaltering,
And faces bold and unashamed
   As in our Christian spring." [1]

But St Paul is again dictating, and we must follow. He has confessed and affirmed, once for all, his standing and fixity in the Lord, and in Him alone. Now he must emphasize another aspect of the living truth, his progress in the Lord; the non-finality of any given attainment in union with Him.

Ver. 12. +Not as though I had already received+ (*elabon*) the crown of accomplished glory, +or had been already perfected+, with the perfection which shall be when "we shall be like Him, for we shall see Him as He is." +No, I am pressing on+ (*diôkô de*), as on the racer's course, +if indeed+, if as a fact, in blessed finality, +I may seize+ (*katalabô*) +that+ promised crown +with a view to which[2] I was actually+ (*kai*) +seized by Christ Jesus+, when in His mercy He as it were laid violent hands upon me, to pluck me from ruin, and to constrain me into His salvation and His service. Yes, "I press on" to "seize" that crown, with the animating thought that it was on purpose that I might "seize" it that the Lord "seized" me; and that so every stage in the upward and onward course of faith runs straight in the line of His will whose mighty, gracious grasp is on me as I go. +Brethren+,

Ver. 13. (I speak the word of pause and of appeal, as if I could stand by you, and lay my hand upon your arm,) +I+ (*egô*), whatever others may think and do about _them_selves, +do not account myself+ (*emauton*, emphatic like *egô*) +to have seized+ the crown as yet; no, one thing (*en de*)—my thoughts, my purposes, are all concentrated on this *one* thing—+the things behind forgetting+, as one experience after another falls behind me into the past, +and towards the things in front stretching out and onward+ (*epekteinomenos*), like the eager racer, with head thrown forward and body bent towards his object, seeking for more and yet more, in the grace and power of my unchangeable

Ver. 14. Saviour, +goal-ward I press on+ (*kata skopon diôkô*), "not uncertainly," with no faltering or divided aim, +unto+ (*eis*), till I actually touch, +the prize+ (*brabeion*, 1 Cor. ix. 24), the victor's wreath,[3] the prize +of+, offered by, made possible through, +the high call of God+, the voice of His prevailing grace[2] coming from *the heights* (*anô*) of glory and leading the believer at length up thither, +in Christ Jesus+; for through Him comes the "call," and its blessed effect is to unite the "called," the converted, sinner *to* Him, so that he lives here and hereafter in Him. +So let all+

Ver. 15. +us perfect ones+ (*hosoi oun teleioi*), with the perfection not of ideal attainment but of Christian maturity and entirety of experience, +be of this mind+; the "mind" of those who rest in Christ immoveably for their acceptance, and press forward in Christ unrestingly in their obedience, ever discovering fresh causes for humility and for progress, as they keep close to Him. +And if you are diversely+ (*eterôs*) +minded in any thing+, if in any detail of theory or statement you cannot yet see with me, +this also God shall unveil to you+. Sure I am that "the Spirit of God speaketh by me," and that ultimately therefore you will, in submission to Him, see as I have taught you. But I am not therefore commissioned in this matter to denounce and excommunicate; I lay the truth before you, and in love leave it upon your reverent thoughts. +Only, as to+

Ver. 16. +what we have succeeded in reaching+,[5] so far as our insight into Christ has actually gone, up to our full present light in the Gospel, +let us step in the same path+ (*tô autô stoichein*[6]), on the unchanging principles of faith, love, and holiness, and with a watchful desire to cherish to the utmost a holy harmony of spirit and conduct.

Here, in suggestive contrast or complement to the section we studied last, the Christian appears in full and energetic movement, animated with a sacred discontent, repudiating all thought of finality in his conformity to his Lord, and in his actual spiritual condition; running, pressing on, remembering at every step that, although grace is present in power, and glory is in view, still this is the journey, not the home; the race, not the goal;

*Nil actum reputans dum quid sibi restat agendum.*

The passage contains of course much divine teaching in detail. But two main points come up conspicuously "for our learning."

i. We have here a strong, and at the same time a most tender, warning against all approaches to a theoretical "perfectionism." Under that word, as I am well aware, many varieties of opinion in detail may be found. And again, few who hold opinions commonly called perfectionist like the word "perfectionism." But I speak with practical accuracy when I give that title to such views as on the whole affirm the attainableness here below of a spiritual condition in which man needs no longer confess himself as now a sinner, and in which his attention tends to be drawn more to his perfectness than to his imperfections of condition. That such views are held, and strongly held, by many earnest Christians, is a familiar fact. As far as my own observation goes, such views are not uncommonly attended, in those who hold them, by a certain oblivion to personal shortcomings and inconsistencies; by an obscuration of consciousness, and of conscience, more or less marked, towards the sinfulness of ordinary, everyday violations of the law of holiness in respect of "meekness, humbleness of mind, longsuffering," sympathy, and other quiet graces.

In the present passage the Apostle's whole spirit moves in just the opposite direction. His complete repose in Christ as the Righteousness of God for him, and then his deep nearness to his Lord as the Power of God in him, alike seem not so much to banish as utterly to preclude any thought about himself but that of his own imperfection. He writes as one whose very last feeling is that of complacency in his spiritual condition. I deliberately do not say "self-complacency"; for all Christians would repudiate that word; I say, complacency in his spiritual condition. His spiritual *position*, in Christ, as he is "found in Him," fills him with much more than complacency; it is his glory and his boast. But when he comes to speak of his spiritual *condition*, the possessing thought is that all is imperfect and progressive. He has a perfect blessing; but he is an imperfect recipient of it; he has "not attained." He is deeply happy. But he is thoroughly humble. As we read the passage, we feel very sure that the man who wrote it would lie very tenderly and candidly open to reproofs, and to painful truths told him about himself. For his Lord, he is ready to bear rejoicing witness to the whole world. For himself, even as in Christ, he holds no brief; nay, he takes the other part.

He has had a vision of absolute holiness which has completely guarded him from the delusion of thinking that he is himself absolutely holy, even in the fullest state of grace. He is so genuinely "perfect" in the sense of mature knowledge of his Lord that he is incapable of thinking himself "perfected."

All the while, this does not for a moment leave him in the miserable plight of acquiescing in sin because he knows he is still a sinner. If he were merely going by a theory, it might be so. But he is going by the Lord Jesus Christ; he is using HIM, daily and hourly, as not only his always abasing standard, but as "all his salvation, and all his desire"; as the infinitely blissful Object of his affections and of his knowledge; as his *Summum Bonum*. While Christ is fully this to the Christian, he will be little likely on the one hand to say, "I am perfect" (Job ix. 20); on the other he will be always seeking, in the most practical of all ways, watching, praying, believing, for a closer conformity and yet closer (*summorphixomenos*) to his Lord's bright image.

And at the back of all his thoughts about defect and progress will lie the restful certainties to which no ideas of defect attach, and from which the idea of progress is absent, because it is out of place—the certainties of the Righteousness of God, "of peace with God through our Lord Jesus Christ"; the being "found in Him."

ii. The passage puts very distinctly before us the thought of the Reward of Grace. The writer is living, loving, working, in view of a "prize," *brabeion*: he looks forward to the Master's hand as it will extend the wreath of victory, and to His voice as it will utter the longed-for words, "Well done, good and faithful Servant." This same man has laboured, in many an hour of public and private teaching, and in many an inspired page, to emphasize the magnificent truth that grace is grace; that God owes man nothing; that "all things are of God"; that "to him that worketh not, but believeth on Him that justifieth the ungodly, his faith is reckoned for righteousness." He well knows that there is a side of truth from which the one possible message is the Lord's own solemn question and answer (Luke xvii. 9), "Doth he thank that servant? I trow not." The most complete and laborious service cannot possibly outrun the obligation of the rescued bondservant to the Possessor, of the limb to the blessed Head. But then, this absolute servitude is to One who is, as a fact, eternal Love. The work is done for a Master who, while His claims are absolute, is such that He personally delights in every response of love to His love, of will to His will. His servant *cannot* serve Him with a grateful heart without thereby pleasing the heart of his Lord. And so, at the close of the day's work, while, from the side of law and claims, the Lord "doth not thank that servant," from the side of love and of moral sympathy He will welcome him in with "Well done, good and faithful servant; enter thou into the joy of thy Lord." And that holy "prize" does, and must, prove a magnet to the Christian's will and hopes. What is he looking for? Not an accession of personal dignity in heaven, but a word from his beloved Master's heart. There is nothing mercenary in this. True, it "has respect unto the recompense of reward." But the "reward" is what only love can give, and only love can take. It is love's approval of the service of love.

Much discussion has been spent upon the theory of reward, in the matter of our service rendered to "our King who has saved us." The theme no doubt is one which admits of much interesting and important enquiry; and it has many sides. But after all the true philosophy of it lies in "the truth as it is *in Jesus.*" Let the Christian be seeking the reward of personal aggrandizement in heaven, "to sit on His right hand, or on His left, in His glory"; and the motive is as earthly as if the scene of its fulfilment were to be an earthly palace. Let him be seeking the "well done" of Jesus Christ, because Jesus Christ has redeemed him, and is dear to him; and he is in the line of the will, and of the love, of God.

[1] Dr H. Bonar.

[2] *Heth ô katelêphthên*: grammatically we may render, "inasmuch as I was seized"; cp. the Greek of Rom. v. 12; 1 Cor. v. 4. But the connexion of thought seems to be best met by the above rendering, which is practically that of A.V. and R.V.

[3] *Stephanos*, as in 1 Cor. ix. 25, Rev. iii. 11, and often. *Stephanos* is properly the victor's wreath, *diadêma* the king's crown (Rev. xix. 12).—For a short essay on St Paul's use of athletic metaphors see this Epistle in *The Cambridge Greek Testament*, Appendix.

[4] *Klêsis, kalein, klêtoi*, in the Epistles will be found regularly to refer not to the general *invitations* of the Gospel, but to the actually prevailing power of God over the wills of His people. See particularly 1 Cor. i. 23, 24, where the "call" is clearly distinguished from the general proclamation, which alas so many "Greeks" and "Jews" heard, but only to reject it.

[5] *Hephthasamen*: the verb seems always to indicate not merely reaching, but reaching *with some difficulty*. I attempt to express this in the translation.

[6] There is good evidence for omitting the words *kanoni, to auto phronein.*—*Stoichein* is more in detail than *peripatein*: "to *step*," not only "to walk." See the Greek of Rom. iv. 12.

"Sovereign Lord and gracious Master,
Thou didst freely choose Thine own,
Thou hast call'd with holy calling,
Thou wilt save, and keep from falling;
Thine the glory, Thine alone!
Yet Thy hand shall crown in heaven
All the grace Thy love hath given;
Just, though undeserv'd, reward
From our glorious, gracious Lord."
F. R. HAVERGAL.

# THE BLESSED HOPE AND ITS POWER

"We are waiting, we are yearning for Thy voice
Through the long, long summer day and winter night;
We are mourning till Thou bid'st our souls rejoice,
 Till Thy coming turns our darkness into light:
  Come, Lord Jesus, come again;
  We shall see Thee as Thou art,
   Then, and not till then,
  In Thy glory bear a part;
   Then, and not till then,
  Thou wilt satisfy each heart."
  J. DENHAM SMITH.

# CHAPTER X

PHILIPPIANS iii. 17-21

The problem of the body—Cautions and tears—"That blessed hope"—The
duty of warning—The moral power of the hope—The hope full of
immortality—My mother's life—"He is able"—The promise of his coming

The Apostle draws to the close of his appeal for a true and watchful fidelity to
the Gospel. He has done with his warning against Judaistic legalism. He has
expounded, in the form of a personal confession and testimony, the true
Christian position, the acceptance of the believer in "the righteousness which
is of God by faith," and the sanctification of the believer through union with
his Lord and in an always growing communion with Him. Throughout this
deep and most tender argument has run everywhere the truth with which it
began, that the sure antidote to the spiritual errors in question is "joy in the
Lord." The glad use of Jesus Christ in His personal glory and perfection, as
He merited for us, and as we abide in Him—this is the way.

Already another class of mistake and danger has risen before his mind, and
occupies it now exclusively. From ver. 12 onward, if I read the passage aright,
he has been thinking not of the legalist only, who opposed and denounced his
doctrine of grace and faith, but of the school or schools which rather would
applaud it—and then distort it. There was the teacher who would assert a
premature and delusive personal perfection, proclaiming himself so close to
Christ that he had already reached the holy goal. And there was the teacher
who would reason so upon the perfectness of the atoning merits as to disclaim
the need of seeking with all his soul a personal conformity to the Lord of the
Atonement. Such a man would conceivably affirm for himself an experience
of intense spiritual insight, a communion with God profound and direct, an
exaltation into a celestial atmosphere of consciousness; while yet, and on his
own avowed theory, he was living a life in which sin was allowed to reign in
his mortal body, What did it matter? The spirit soared and expatiated in a
higher region. The true man lived in the world above, "commercing with the
skies"; it was but the body, soon to perish, which went its own way, and might
be allowed to do so, for it could never be other than the uncongenial burthen
of the real man.

Such theories, as all are aware, were largely developed and widely spread in
the sub-apostolic age. The word Gnosticism, so familiar to the reader of the

89

early history of thought in and around the Church, reminds us of this; for while many Gnostics were severe ascetics, others were practical libertines; and the divergent practices sprang from one deep source of error, dishonour of the body. To both schools, spirit was good, matter was evil. By both therefore the body was viewed not as a subject of redemption, but as a barrier in its way. The one aimed to wear out the barrier, to help it to disappear. The others left it, as they thought, alone; leapt, as they thought, over it; as if they could pursue a spiritual life which should be irrespective of the body's hopeless evils.

The embryo, at least, of this latter type of thought was beyond doubt apparent in St Paul's day, and had begun to be felt at Philippi. There, in that loving and beloved community, the plague had begun, or at least the infection was imminent. "Many walked" (perhaps not actually at Philippi yet, but they might soon come) in the foul broad road which they asserted to be clean and narrow. Very probably they used the terms of the Pauline Gospel, and said much of grace, and faith, and the Spirit, and the things above. But none the less they were the victims of an awful self-delusion; teachers whose doctrine led downwards to the pit. To them he comes at length, explicitly and finally. In view of them he places before the Philippians once more the fact of his own and his brethren's examples, and then the sanctifying power of that blessed hope, the Redemption of the Body.

Ver. 17. +United imitators of me become ye, brethren+; taking me, your long-known guide in the Lord, for your moral pattern, and strengthening your mutual cohesion (*summimêtai*) by so doing (an appeal prompted not by egotism or self-confidence, but by single-hearted certainty about my message and my purpose); +and mark+, watch, in order to tread in their steps,[1] +those who so walk as you have us+, me and my missionary-brethren, +for a model+; those whose practical conduct in human life and intercourse (*peripatein*), seen among you day by day in its wholesomeness and truth, plainly reproduces what you remember of ours. There is need for this attention, and for this

Ver. 18. discrimination. +For there are many men walking+, pursuing a line of conduct and practice, +whom I often used to tell you of+, in the days of our direct intercourse, +but+ (*de*) +now tell you of actually+ (*kai*) +with cries and tears+ (*klaiôn*), (so much has the evil grown, in extent and in depth, so awfully apparent are its issues, for this world and the world to come,) +as the enemies+, *the* personal enemies (*tous echthrous*), as if in a bad pre-eminence, +of the Cross of our+ (*tou*) +Christ+, that Cross of whose virtues they can say much, but whose power upon the soul they utterly ignore; +of+

Ver. 19. +whom the end is perdition+, ruin of the whole being,[2] final and hopeless; +of whom the god is the belly+, (the sensual appetites, the body's degradation, not its function,) while they claim an exalted and special intimacy with the Supreme; +and their+ (*he*) +glory+, their boast to see deeper and to soar higher than others, +is in their shame; men whose mind is for+ (*phronouten*) +the things on earth+, not, as they dream, or as at least they say, for the things of an upper and super-corporeal world. No; their subtle doctrine of spirit and body—what is it when tested in its issues? It is but a philosophy of sin; a gossamer robe over the self-indulgence which has come to be the real interest of the theorist, the real occupation of his will. All is really, with them, of the earth, earthy. Far other is the doctrine we have learned, and have striven to exemplify, at the feet of Christ.

Ver. 20. For our city-home, the seat of our citizenship, and of the conduct which it demands and inspires,[3] +subsists in the heavens+, is always there, an antecedent and abiding fact (*huparchei*), on which we are to act in life; in that heavenly world, where the Lord is, and for which He is training us; the eternal Country of this eternal City and Home; +out of which+ (city)[4] +we are actually+ (*kai*) +waiting for, as our Saviour+, in the full and final sense, the +Lord Jesus Christ, who will+

Ver. 21. +transfigure+—not annihilate, not cast away as essentially evil, but wonderfully change in its conditions, and so in its guise, in its semblance (*schêma*)—+the body of our humiliation+, this body, now inseparably connected with the burthens and abasements of our mortality, *humbling* us continually in the course of its necessities, and of its sufferings, but not therefore, in its essence, other than God's good handiwork; +to be conformed+, with a resemblance based on an essential assimilation (*summorphon, morphê*), +to the body of His glory+, as He resumed His blessed Body when He rose, and as He wears it now upon the Throne, and in it manifests Himself to the happy ones in their bliss; +according to+, in ways and measures conditioned only by, +the forth-putting+ (*energeia*) +of His ability actually to subdue to Himself all things that are+ (*ta panta*).

So the great passage, the pregnant chapter, ends. As it began so it closes—with Jesus Christ. With Him His servant can never have done; "Him first, Him midst, Him last, and without end." Jesus Christ is the present joy, and the everlasting hope. His perfected righteousness is the believer's actual deep safety and repose. His unsearchable riches of personal grace and glory are the constant animation and ever-rising standard of the believer's spiritual progress. He is the eternal Antidote to our fears, and also to our sins. He is the infinite Contradiction to the least compromise, under any pretext, with evil; and He is this, among other ways, by being Himself "that blessed Hope"; "the Lord Jesus Christ, which is our Hope" (1 Tim. i. 1); so that the prospect of

His Return, and of what He will do for us, and for Himself (*eautô*), when He returns, is to be our mighty motive in the matter of practical, aye of bodily, cleanness and holiness of life.

The whole passage now before us is strongly characteristic of the New Testament way of dealing with sin. In the first place, there is no lack of urgent and explicit warning. The moral and spiritual evil is labelled unmistakably. It is pointed out as a danger not hypothetical but actual; not floating in the air, but embodied in lives and influences: "*Many persons walk* whom I tell you of with tears as the enemies of the cross of Christ." And of these persons, as such, it is unflinchingly said that their end is *atôleia*, "ruin," "perdition"; dread and hopeless word. In all this lies a lesson for our day. In many quarters the solemn utterance of warning is now almost silent; it is regarded as almost unchristian to warn sinners, even open sinners, to do anything so much out of the fashion as "to flee from the wrath to come," "the wrath which is coming upon the children of disobedience." But this is not the apostolic way, nor the Lord's way.

Yet this passage, this heart-searching appeal, while it deals with warning, does not end with it. Its strongest and chosen argument is not fear but hope; not perdition but "the coming again of our Lord Jesus Christ, and our gathering together unto Him." St Paul has to guard the Philippians against a most subtle form of sensual temptation, a masterpiece of the Enemy. In passing, and with bitter tears, he points to the gulph where that path ends. In closing, and with his whole heart, he points to the coming Lord in His benignant glory, and to the unutterable joy of our being then, finally and even in our material being, transfigured for ever into His likeness.

For our own blessing, and for that of others, let us follow this example. Whether in the pulpit to a listening throng, or in more individual approaches to other men, or when we turn in upon ourselves, and, like the Psalmists, speak to our own souls, in the most secret possible hour, let us seek to speak thus. Let us not take an opiate against the ideas of judgment, wrath, perdition —unless, with our Bibles quite open, we are quite sure that such things are only dreams of a past religious night. Let us take urgent heed, above all for ourselves, lest we *lose faith in the warnings* of God. But all the while let us present to ourselves, and to others, as the great argument of all for saying "No" to specious sin, "that blessed Hope." Let us consider Jesus Christ, till He shines upon us in something of the glory of His Person and His Work. Let us wait for Him from heaven. More and more, as the years roll, and the suns set, and "that day" is approaching, let us take our place among those who "love His appearing." And as for our bodies, and His call to be pure in body as in spirit, let us continually remember that "the body is for the Lord, and the

Lord for the body" (1 Cor. vi. 13). Let us not merely try to reason down temptation, or to order it down, in the name of abstract rightness, or of concrete peril. Let us recollect as a glorious fact that the body is the purchased property of the Lord Jesus; that He cares for it, as His dear-bought possession; that He can, by His own Spirit, sanctify it now, through and through; and that He is coming, perhaps very soon indeed, to "transfigure it to be conformed to the body of His glory."

The whole genius of the Gospel tends to connect together, as closely as possible, holiness and happiness. They are to act and react in manifold ways in the Christian life. Holiness lies at the root of happiness, as its deep condition. But also happiness, from another point of view, waters the root of holiness, and expands its flowers, and brings its sweet fruit to fulness. "The joy of the Lord is your strength"—your strength to say to temptation a "No" which shall be entirely willing and simple. Never shall we so tread down the tempter, and the traitor, as when we are "rejoicing in Christ Jesus," and "in the hope of the glory of God."

Then let us cultivate this blessed secret. Let us prove the power of Christ loved and looked for. In a very special sense let St Paul teach us here to apply to our present needs the force of a heavenly future, the future of His coming, and of our meeting Him and being transfigured by Him. In many directions, in the Church, this rule is being practised now with great earnestness, and with happy issues; the looking for the Lord's Return is indeed a reality to many. But in many directions it is otherwise. Christian thought and labour too often seem to limit themselves to the sphere of the present, and to forget that the goal of the Gospel is not a state of social *bien-être* developed by philanthropy under the auspices, so to speak, of Christ, but an immortality of holy power and service, won for us by His merits, prepared for us by His exaltation, while we are prepared for it by His Spirit working in us. Again and again we need to remember this. The Gospel showers along its path, upon the mortal life of man, personal and social blessings of the philanthropic kind which nothing else can possibly bring down. It makes to-day infinitely important by connecting it with the eternal to-morrow. But the path is towards that to-morrow. "We look at the things not seen, for the things which are not seen are eternal." We "desire a better country, that is, an heavenly." "It doth not yet appear what we shall be; we shall be like Him, for we shall see Him as He is."

Much current Christian teaching practically tends to drop immortality very nearly out of sight. The Lord's Return, the heavenly Life, "the liberty of the glory of the sons of God"—these topics are either little mentioned, or treated too much as luxuries and ornaments of the Gospel. But it was not so for the

Lord Jesus, and for His Apostles. And we shall find that to follow Him and them in this, as in other things, is best. It "hath the promise of the life that now is, and of that which is to come." Their doctrine of the future is much more than an antidote to death. It is the mighty animation of life. It makes altogether for present purity, and righteousness, and self-sacrificing love, in the concrete circumstances of this generation. It is the thought in which alone man can live his true life *now*, as a being who is made "to glorify God—and to enjoy Him fully *for ever*."

As a matter of fact, no human life is so true, full, and beautiful as that which is at once assiduously attentive to present duty and service, and full of the everlasting hope. Such lives are being lived all around us. Which of my readers has not known at least one such? For me, one among many shines out in my heart radiant with a brightness all its own; it is the life of my blessed Mother. She has now been a great while with the Lord, on whom she so long believed. But the impression of what that "conversation" was is not only indelible; it lives and moves, as fresh to-day as ever. It was a busy life—the life of a wife, a mother of many sons, a friend of many friends, the pastor's help-mate in a poor parish. It was a life of minute and devoted attention to every duty, large and little. It was a life of warm and ready sympathies, and manifold interests. But it was a life all the while of divine communion, and of an unwavering "hope full of immortality." Dear to that heart indeed were husband, children, friends, neighbours, suffering and sinning world. Very fruitful was that life for individual and social blessing, just such as the philanthropist seeks to convey. Side by side with my Father, who laboured incessantly through a long life for God and man, and for men's health as well as their salvation, my Mother lived for others in all their present needs. But the springs of what she was, and did, were within the veil. And the choice and the longing were always, in perfect harmony with every strong human affection, directed towards heaven She did indeed "wait, as for her Saviour, for the Lord Jesus Christ." And the whole result, for those whom that life affected, was a deep, strong evidence of Christianity. In her we saw the Gospel beautify the present by lifting the veil of the blessed future. We recognized the reality of Jesus Christ now by converse with one who so much desired the sight of His glory *then*.

As we draw to an end, let us take up the closing words of our paragraph, and read them as a special "lesson of faith." St Paul is telling us of a change yet to pass over us, over these our bodies, altogether inconceivable in kind and degree. They are to be "transfigured into conformity to the body of our Saviour's glory." Yes, it is inconceivable; in modern parlance, it is "unthinkable." "How can these things be?" Well, Scripture does not invite us to "conceive" it, to "think" it, in the sense of thinking it out. It helps us indeed elsewhere (1 Cor. xv.) with intimations and illustrations, up to a certain point; but this is not to explain, or to ask us to explain. What it does is something better; it invites us to trust a personal Agent, who understands all that He has undertaken, and who is able. "How can these things be?" Not according to this or that law, principle, or tendency, which we can divine. No; but "according to the mighty working whereby HE is able to subdue all things unto Himself."

The method of the Bible is to give us ample views of what Jesus Christ is, and then (not before) to ask us to trust Jesus Christ to DO what he says He can. He says, "I will raise you up at the last day." And He does not go on to explain. He says nothing in detail of His *modus operandi*. We are in absolute ignorance of it, as much as the Christians of five, or ten, or eighteen centuries ago. We do not know how. But we know Him. And He has said, "I will"—and has died and risen again.

Shall we not rest here? It is good ground. "I know whom I have believed; and am persuaded that He is able."

And what is true of His power and promise in this great matter of our resurrection and our glory, is true of course all round the circle of His undertakings. "He can subdue all things." And therefore, not only death, and the grave, and the mysteries of matter, but also our hearts, our affections, our wills. He can "bring every thought into captivity" to the holy rule of His thought. He can "subdue our iniquities." And he can subdue also all that we know as circumstance and condition; making the crooked straight, and the rough places plain. How, we may be wholly ignorant beforehand; only, "according to the mighty working."

Lastly, it is *heautô*,[5] "unto HIMSELF." What a word of rest and power! Our expectation of His victories in us and for us does not terminate upon ourselves; it is never safe to terminate things there. It rises and rests in Himself. Our glorification, body and soul, is, ultimately, "unto Him"; therefore the prospect, and the desire, are boundlessly right and safe. "To subdue all things *unto Himself*"; so as to serve Him, to promote His ends, to do His will. Our absolute emancipation from all the limitations of both moral and material evil is "unto Himself." Emancipation on this side, it is an entire and eternal annexation on the other. The being will be fully liberated that it may fully serve—"day and night in His temple."

"Even so, come, Lord Jesus." Come, to our full and final salvation. Come, that we, the beings whom Thou hast made, and remade, may enjoy "the liberty of the glory" (Rom. viii. 21) for which we were destined in Thy love. Come, that we may be for ever happy, and strong, and free, in that wonderful world of the resurrection. Come, that we may meet again with exceeding joy the beloved ones who have gone before us, and all Thy saints, and may with them inherit the everlasting kingdom. But oh come yet more for Thyself, and for Thy glory, and to take Thy full possession. "Subdue all things," Lord Jesus, "unto Thyself." Subdue our death for ever, that our endless life may be, in all its fulness, spent for Thee.

"For Thou hast met our longings
With words of golden tone,
That we shall serve for ever
Thyself, Thyself alone;

"Shall serve Thee, and for ever,
Oh hope most sure, most fair;
The perfect love outpouring
In perfect service there." [6]

[1] *skopeite*: *skopein* usually has reference to the attention which results in avoidance; so Rom. xvi. 17: *parakalô skopein tous ta skandala poiountas kai ekklinate k.t.l.* But here obviously the "looking" is for imitation.—The Philippians knew St Paul's teaching, and in his attached leading disciples among them they could *see* it embodied.

[2] Cp. Matt. vii. 13; Rom. vi. 21; 2 Cor. xi. 15; Heb. vi. 8; 1 Pet. iv. 17.

[3] I thus attempt to give the meaning of *politeuma*, so far as I understand it. The R.V. renders it *"citizenship,"* and *"commonwealth"* in the margin. The usage of the word in Greek literature amply justifies either, and either well suits the general context. The Apostle means that Christians are citizens of the heavenly City as to their *status*, and are therefore "obliged by their nobility" to live, however far from their home, as those who belong to it, and represent it. What seems lacking however in the rendering of the R.V. is the idea of *locality*, which (to me) was clearly present to St Paul's mind in his use of *politeuma* here. The proof of this lies in the words *ex ou* just below; not *ex ôn* (*ouranôn*) but *ex ou* (*politeumatos*): I can find *no proof* of the assertion (Moulton's *Winer*, p. 177) that *ex ou* is a mere equivalent for *hothen*, and so may refer to the plural *ouranoi*. The rendering *"seat* of citizenship" seems fairly to represent *politeuma* thus.—The A.V. *"conversation"* (Lat. *conversatio*, "intercourse of life") probably represents an impression of the translators that the Apostle is as it were echoing i. 27, *axiôs tu euaggeliou politeuesthe*. But the imagery here is different, and definite.

[4] See note just above on *ex ou*.

[5] Perhaps read *auta*. But the translation must remain the same.

[6] F. R. Havergal.

# PURITY AND PEACE IN THE PRESENT LORD

"Now the Christians, O King, as men who know God, ask from Him petitions which are proper for Him to give and for them to receive; and thus they accomplish the course of their lives. And because they acknowledge the goodnesses of God towards them, lo! on account of them there flows forth the beauty that is in the world."—*Apology of Aristides, about* A.D. 130; *translated by* MRS RENDEL HARRIS.

# CHAPTER XI

PHILIPPIANS iv. 1-9

Euodia and Syntyche—Conditions to unanimity—Great uses of small occasions—Connexion to the paragraphs—The fortress and the sentinel—A golden chain of truths—Joy in the Lord—Yieldingness—Prayer in everything —Activities of a heart at rest

Ver. 1. +So, my brethren beloved and longed for+, *missed* indeed, at this long distance from you, +my joy and crown+ of victory (*stephanos*), +thus+, as having such certainties and such aims, with such a Saviour, and looking for such a heaven, +stand firm in the Lord, beloved ones+.

The words are a link of gold between the passage just ended and that which is to follow. They sum up the third chapter of the Epistle into one practical issue. In view of all that can tempt them away to alien thoughts and beliefs St Paul once more points the converts to Jesus Christ; or rather, he once more bids them remember that in Him they are, and that their safety, their life, is to stay there, recollected and resolved. There is the point of overwhelming advantage against error, and against sin; and only there. "Standing in the Lord," in remembrance and *in use* of their vital union with Him, they would be armed alike against the pharisaic and the antinomian heresy. Counterfeits and perversions would be seen, or at least *felt*, to be such while they were thus in living and working contact with the REALITY. There, with a holy instinct, they would repudiate utterly a merit of their own before God, and a strength of their own against sin. There, with equal inward certainty, they would detect and reject the suggestion that they "should not surely die," though impurity was cloaked and loved.

But the words we have just rendered look forward also. St Paul is about to allude, for the last time, and quite explicitly, to that blot on the fair Philippian fame, the presence in the little mission Church of certain jealousies and divisions. One instance of this evil is prominent in his thoughts, no doubt on Epaphroditus' report. Two Christian women, Euodia[1] and Syntyche, evidently well-known Church members, possibly officials, "deaconesses," like Phoebe (Rom. xvi. 1), were at personal variance. Into their life and work for Christ (for workers they were, or however had been; they had "wrestled along with Paul in the Gospel,") had come this grievous inconsistency. Somehow (modern experiences in religious activity supply illustrations only too easily) they had let the spirit of self come in; jealousy and a sense of grievance lay between them. And out of this unhappy state it was the Apostle's deep desire to bring them, quickly and completely. He appeals to them personally about it, with a directness and explicitness which remind us how homelike still were the conditions of the mission Church. He calls on his "true yoke-fellow," and on Clement, and on his other "fellow-labourers," to "help" the two to a better mind, by all the arts of Christian friendship. But surely first, in this verse, he leads not only the Philippians generally but Euodia and Syntyche in particular up to a level where the self-will and self-assertion must, of themselves, expire. "Stand firm in the Lord." In recollection and faith surround yourselves with Jesus Christ. The more you do so the more you will find that so to be in Him is to "be of one mind in Him." In that PRESENCE self is put to shame indeed. Pique, and petty jealousies, and miserable heart-burnings, and "just pride," die of inanition there, and heart meets heart in love, because in Christ.

It is not guaranteed to us, I think, that we shall certainly be brought here on earth to perfect intellectual agreement by a realized union with Christ all round. Such agreement will certainly be promoted by such a realization; we all know how powerfully, in almost all matters outside number and figure, feeling can influence reasoning; and to have feeling rightly adjusted, "in Him that is true," must be a great aid to just reasoning, and so a great contribution to mental agreement. Thomas Scott, in his *Force of Truth*, (a memorable record of experience,) maintains that vastly more doctrinal concord would be attained in Christendom if all true Christians unreservedly and with a perfect will sought for "God's heart" (and mind) "in God's words."[2] But it is a law of our present state, even in Christ, that "we know in part"; and while this is so, certain discrepancies of inference would seem to be necessary, where many minds work each with its partial knowledge. It is otherwise with "*the spirit* of our mind," the attitude of will and affection in which we think. In the Lord Jesus Christ *this* is meant to be, and can be, rectified indeed, as "every thought is brought into captivity" to Him. If so, to "stand firm in Him" is the way of escape out of all such miseries of dissension (whether between two friends, or two Churches, or two enterprises) as are due not to reasoning but to feeling. "In Him" there is *really* no room for envy, and retaliation, and "the unhappy desire of becoming great," and the eager combat for our own opinion *as such*. "Standing firm in Him" the Euodias and Syntyches of all times and places *must tend* to be of one mind, one attitude of mind (*phronein*). So far as they are, in a sinful sense, not so "minded," it is because they are half out of Him.

But now St Paul comes to them, name by name. What must the tender weight of the words have been as they were first read aloud at Philippi!

Ver. 2. +To Euodia I appeal+ (*parakalô*),[3] +and to Syntyche I appeal, to be of the same mind, in the Lord+; to lay aside differences of feeling, born of self, in the power of their common union in Christ.[5] +Aye+ (read

Ver. 3. *nai*, not *kai*), +and I beg thee also+, thee in *thy* place, as I seek to do in mine, +thou genuine yoke-fellow,[5] help them+ (*autais*)—these sisters of ours thus at variance, +women who+ (*aitines*) +wrestled along with me+, as devoted and courageous workers, +in the+ cause of the +Gospel+, when the first conflicts with the powers of evil were fought at Philippi; yes, do this loving service, +with Clement[6] too, and my other fellow-workers, whose names are in the Book of Life+; the Lord's own, "written in heaven," His for ever.[7]

Wonderful is the great use of small occasions everywhere in Scripture. Minor incidents in a biography are texts for sentences which afford oracles of truth and hope for ever. Local and transitory errors, like that of the Thessalonians about their departed friends, give opportunity for a prophecy on which bereaved hearts are to rest and rejoice till the last trumpet sounds. The unhappy disagreement of two pious women at Philippi is dealt with in words which lead up to the thought of the eternal love of God for His chosen; as if the very unworthiness of the matter in hand, by a sort of repulsion, drove the inspired thought to the utmost height, without for one moment diverting it from its purpose of peace and blessing. And now, in the passage which is to follow, the thought still keeps its high and holy level. It says no more indeed of the Book of Life. But it unfolds in one sentence after another the manifestation here below of the eternal life in all its holy loveliness. It invites Euodia, and Syntyche, and us with them, to the sight of what the believer is called to be, and may be, day by day, as he rejoices in the Lord, and recollects His presence, and tells Him everything as it comes, and so lives "in rest and quietness," deep in His peace; and finds his happy thoughts occupied not with the miseries of self-esteem and self-assertion, but with all that is pure and good, in the smile of the God of peace.

The passage now to be translated has surely this among its other precious attractions and benefits, that it stands related to what has gone just before. The precepts and promises are not given as it were in the air; they are occasioned by Euodia and Syntyche, or rather by what they have suggested to St Paul's mind, the crime and distress of an unchristian spirit in Christians. It is with this he is dealing. And he deals with it not by an elaborate exposure of its obvious wrong, but by carrying it into the sanctuary of holiness and peace, there to die.

With this recollection let us read the words now before us.

Ver. 4. +Rejoice in the Lord always; again I will say+ (*erô*), +Rejoice+; I have said it above, as my antidote-word to every subtle error; I come back (*palin*) to say it again, as my antidote to self-will. Your

Ver. 5. +yieldingness+, your selflessness, the spirit which will yield in *anything* that is only of self, for Christ's sake, +let it be known to all men+, let it be proved a reality in real life, by all and sundry who have to do with you; +the Lord is near+, always beside you, to

Ver. 6. know, to love, to elevate, to calm.[8] +About nothing be anxious+ (*merimnate*); *never* let yourselves be burthened and distracted *as those who are alone from your Lord*; +but in everything+, however great, however little, +by your+ (*tê*) +prayer+, your whole worshipping approach to Him, +and your+ (*tê*) +supplication+, your definite petitions of Him, +with thanksgiving+, thanks at least for this, that you have Him to speak to and to trust, +let your requests be made known towards our God+ (*pros ton Theon*), with perfect simplicity of detail, putting aside all the mysteries of prayer in the

Ver. 7. recollection that He bids you pray. +And+, and thus, not anyhow, but thus, in adoring, trusting communion with Him, +the peace of God+, the innermost tranquillity caused by contact with Him, breathed by His Spirit into ours, the peace +which transcends all mind+, for no reasoning can explain and define its nature and its consciousness, +shall+ (it is nothing less than a promise) +safeguard+, as garrison, as sentinel (*phrourêsei*), +your hearts+, in all their depths of will, affection, and reflexion, +and your thoughts+, the very workings of those hearts in detail, +in Christ Jesus+. In Him you are, as your Fortress of rest and holiness; and, while there you rest, this sacred keeper watches the door; the peace of God is sentinel.

Such was to be the condition for the true play of the inner life; such, not in a dream but at Philippi, were to be their "hearts and thoughts, in Christ Jesus"; thus happy, gentle, unanxious, prayerful, thankful, all the day. And now, what is to be the matter for such conditions, the food for such thinking and such willing? There is to be no vacuum, called peace. These "hearts and thoughts" are to be active, discursive, reflective; "reckoning," "calculating," "reasoning out" (*logixesthai*) innumerable things—all with a view, of course, to the life-long work of serving God and man.

Ver. 8. For, +finally, brethren, all things that are true, all things that are honourable+, serious, sacred, venerable, self-respectful, +all things that are righteous+, as between man and man in common life, +all things that are pure+, clean words, clean deeds, +all things that are amiable+, gracious, kindly; for manner as well as matter falls under the will of God; +all things that are sweet to speak of+, things prompting a loving and noble tone of conversation; +whatever virtue there is+, truly so called, not in the pagan sense of self-grounded vigour, even in right directions, but in that of the energy for right which is found in God; +and whatever praise there is+, given rightly by the human conscience to deeds and purposes of good; +these things think out+, reckon, reason on (*logixesthe*). Let *right* in all its practical, all its noble forms, be the subject-matter of your considering and designing activities within. Strong, not in yourselves but in your Lord's presence and His peace, use His strength in you to work out every precept of His Word, every whisper of His Spirit, every dictate of the conscience He has given.

Then follows one word of a more personal kind; it is no egotism, but as if he would remind them amidst these great generalities of principle that they well knew a human life which strove to realize them in practice.

Ver. 9. +The things you learnt+ of me, +and received+ as revealed truth from me, and +heard and saw in me, these things practise+ (*prassette*), make them the habits of your lives; and so +the God of peace+, Author and Giver of peace within, and of harmony around, +shall be with you+; your Companion and Guardian, "Lord of the Sabbath" of the soul, secret of the true unity of the group, and of the Church.

Thus we read over again this golden chain of "commandments which are not grievous" and "exceeding precious promises." Few passages of equal length, even in St Paul's Epistles, at once invite more attention to details of language and convey richer spiritual messages. Very passingly and partially I have noted the more important details of word and phrase, in the course of the translation. It remains to say not what I would but what I can, in brief compass, upon the messages to the Christian's soul.

Let us be quite practical, and let our study take the simplest form. In this wonderful paragraph let us not only wonder; let us take its sentences as revelations of fact. Here the Holy Spirit through the Apostle sets before us some of the intended facts of the normal Christian life. These precepts were not meant to dissolve into bright dreams; they were to be obeyed in Philippi then, and in England now; they were spoken for not ideal but actual human beings, the rank and file of the followers of the Lord. These promises were not meant to be met with an aspiration, followed by a sigh. They were to be received and used, as certainties of the grace of God, "before the sons of men."

Come then to the paragraph once again, to study it with real life in immediate view, and in the full consciousness of our own sin and weakness. Here are some of the normal "possibilities of grace," not for the strong and holy but for the very weak, for those who know that "in their flesh dwelleth no good thing," but who come to Jesus, and (if only for very fear and need) stay by Him.

Here then is the fact, first, that the Christian life, as such, is to be, and may be, a life of "joy in the Lord always." Such is "the Lord" that He is indeed able to be a perpetual cause of joy. The believer has but to recollect HIM, to consider HIM, to converse with HIM, to make use of HIM, in order to have in himself (not *of* himself) "a well of water, springing up unto eternal life." "In joy and sorrow, life and death, His love is still the same"; for HE is still the same; and the believing man is His.

He will henceforth covet, and cultivate, this life of holy "joy in the Lord always." It is not a boisterous mirth; it is pure and chastened; but it *is joy*. It is an unfigurative happiness, a deep practical cheerfulness, full of health for him who has it, and a most powerful secret for influence over those who have to do with him. Think of the track of light left behind by lives of holy joy which we have watched! It was good to be near them. The very things and places round them were warmed and beautified by them. And their source and strength lay, not in the believer, but in "the Lord"; therefore the way is open for us too; we may be bearers of such sunshine too, happy and making happy.

"By influence of the light divine
Let thy own light to others shine;
Reflect all heaven's propitious rays
In ardent love and cheerful praise." [9]

Again, here is the fact that the normal Christian life is, as such, a life of "moderation known unto all men," in the controlling calm of the nearness of the Lord. The meaning of this "moderation" (*to epieikes*) we have seen; it is that blessed facility, that unselfish yieldingness, which is not weakness at all but the outcome of the meekness of a heart which Christ has overcome. It is the instinctive spirit, where He is in full command of thought and will, when personal "grievances" cross us, when our personal claims are slighted, our feelings disregarded, and even our legitimate rights overridden. Of course more considerations than one have to be taken as to our action when our rights are overridden. We have to ask whether our yielding will be helpful or hurtful *to others*; we have even to ask whether to yield may not do harm to the invader. But these questions, if honestly asked, stand clear of the spirit of self; they regard others. And wherever they can be so answered as to leave us free to yield in view of others, we, if Christians indeed, living really our Christian life, shall find it quite possible, in the Lord Jesus, to let our "yieldingness be known unto all men," in the deep calm of "the Lord at hand." Yes, this can be so, in the most complicated life, and with the most irritable character, if we will fully "receive the grace of God" (2 Cor. vi. 1). And the "all men" who "know" it will note it, and will recognize, sooner or later, the Master in the servant.

Yet again, the normal Christian life is given here as a life free from care, from that miserable anxiety, *merimna*, which blights and withers human happiness far and wide, whether it comes in the form of a weight of large responsibilities or of the most trifling misgivings. "Be careful for nothing"; "care-ful" in the antique sense of the word; "burthened with care." In the modern sense of careful, no one should be more careful than we; "faithful in the least," "shewing all good fidelity in all things," "walking circumspectly," accurately, *akribôs* (Eph. v. 15), "pleasing the neighbour for his good unto edification," "whether we eat or drink, doing all to the glory of God," "watching and praying always." But in the other sense we are, we positively are, enjoined to live "without carefulness"; to take pains, but in peace; to work and serve, but at rest within; to "provide," to think beforehand (*pronoeisthai*, Rom. xii. 17), but in the repose of soul given by the fact that with the morrow will come the Lord, or rather that He will walk with us and lead us into it. It is a great triumph to live such a life; but it is His triumph, not ours. Let us leave Him free (may the word be used in reverence?) to win it; to "do this mighty work," to "bear our burthen daily" (so we may render Ps. lxxviii. 19). Nothing will much more glorify Him in eyes that notice our daily walk than to see us always taking care, yet always unanxious while we take it.

"In the calm of sweet communion
Let thy daily work be done;
In the peace of soul-outpouring
Care be banish'd, patience won." [10]

The sweet hymn leads us straight to the next point. The normal Christian life, according to this paragraph, is a life of perpetual, habitual, converse with God, converse about everything. And such converse has everything to do with the unanxious life. The man who would be unanxious is to cultivate the practice of reverent, worshipping (*proseuchê*), thankful, *detailed prayer*; so shall he enter into peace. Here is a large subject; it is inexhaustible; from every aspect prayer is wonderful; and there are many kinds and types of prayer, as regards the act and exercise of it. But the all-important thing to remember here is that we are called *to pray* as the great means to a divine unanxious peace; and that we are called to pray in the sense of "making our requests known *in everything*." Shall we, in the grace of God, set ourselves to do it? Shall we remember the presence of the Hearer, and "practise the Presence"? Shall we act upon it? More, and more, and always more, shall we really "*in everything*" turn to Him, and tell Him? Thought is good, but prayer is better; or rather, thought in the form of prayer is, in ten thousand cases, the best thought. Let us make it a rule, God helping, "in everything" which calls for pause, for consideration, for judgment, to pray first and then to think. Innumerable futile thoughts will thus be saved, thoughts made fruitless by a hurry of spirit, or a heat, or a hardness, which puts all our view out of order. We shall indeed need to take pains. For while nothing is simpler in idea than the act of speaking to the unseen Friend, nothing is more easy, alas, to let slip in practice. But the pains will be infinitely worth the while; it will be all applied at the right point. Wonderful result, guaranteed here by the Hearer of prayer; His "peace shall safeguard our hearts and our thoughts, in Christ Jesus," in the living Sanctuary of security and strength. There all our powers shall be active, yet at rest; dealing with a thousand things, yet always conditioned by Him who is "the One Thing Needful." Unity will lie at the heart of multiplicity; Christ will rule life from the centre.

Lastly, the normal Christian life, thus conditioned, is a life whose mental energies (*logixesthe*) are fully at work, always gravitating towards purposes and actions true, pure, gracious, virtuous, commendable; "sowing the fruit of righteousness in peace," at the side of "the God of peace." True, the man may have many things to think of which are either perfectly secular in themselves (he may be a servant, he may be a man of business, he may be a physician, he may be a minister of state); or which are evil in themselves (he may be an investigator, or a judge, of crime). Nevertheless, this will not deflect the true current of the mind. These "thinkings" will all find place and direction in the "thought" which remembers that the thinker is the Lord's, and that in his *whole* life he is to be true to the Lord's glory and the good of man. "The God of peace will be with him" wherever he goes, whatever he does; deep below the surface, but so as to control the whole surface all the while.

Such is the Christian life, where the Christian "stands firm in the Lord." It was thus at Philippi. In the early generations of the Church (let the *Apology of Aristides* alone be adequate witness) it was thus, to a degree and to an extent most memorable, in at least very many Christian circles. It is thus still, in many an individual life. But is it in any sense whatever thus in the rule and average or even earnest Christian lives? Is it thus in ours?

"Henceforth, let us *live*—not unto ourselves, but unto Him who died for us, and rose again." To Him, in Him, by Him, we are bound to live so (Rom. viii. 12, *opheileta*), we are able to live so. Let us "present ourselves to God" (Rom. vi. 13), watching and praying, and it shall be.

"Two arms I find to hold Thee fast,
Submission meek and reverent faith;
Held by Thy hand that hold shall last
Through life and over death.

"Not me the dark foe fears at all,
But hid in Thee I take the field;
Now at my feet the mighty fall,

For Thou hast bid them yield." [11]

[1] So certainly read, not *Euodias*, which would be a man's name, a contraction of Euodianus. Euodias as a fact is not found in inscriptions. Euodia on the other hand is a known feminine name; and the words just following ("help these women") make it practically certain that the two persons just named were both female converts. (*Euodian* of course may be the accusative of either *Euodias* or *Euodia*.)

[2] *Cor Dei in verbis Dei*; Gregory the Great's noble description of the Bible, in a letter to the courtier Theodoras, begging him to study daily "the Letter of the heavenly Emperor."

[3] "I exhort," R.V. A slightly tenderer word seems better to represent *parakalein* in this personal connexion. "I beseech" (A.V.) is *perhaps* rather too tender.

[4] "As a curiosity of interpretation, Ellicott (see also Lightfoot, p. 170) mentions the conjecture of Schwegler, that Euodia and Syntyche are really designations of *Church-parties* [the imagined Petrine and Pauline parties], the names being devised and significant [Euodia='*Good-way*,' Orthodoxy; Syntyche='*Combination*,' of Gentiles and Jews on equal terms]. This theory of course regards our Epistle as a fabrication of a later generation, intended as an *eirenicon*. 'What will not men affirm?'" (Note on ver. 2 in *The Cambridge Bible for Schools*).

[5] We know nothing for certain of this person. Lightfoot suggests that it was Epaphroditus, whom St Paul would thus commission not only orally but in writing, as a sort of credential. One curious and most improbable conjecture is that it was *St Paul's wife*. Renan (*Saint Paul*, p. 148) renders here *ma chère épouse*.

[6] Perhaps the bishop of Rome of a later day. So Origen and Eusebius. But we cannot be certain of the identity.

[7] "Cp. Rev. iii. 5, xiii. 8, xvii. 8, xx. 12, 15, xxi. 27; and Luke x. 20. And see Exod. xxxii. 32, 33; Ps. lxix. 28, lxxxvii. 6; Isa. iv. 3; Ezek. xiii. 9; Dan. xii. 1. The result of the comparison of these passages with this seems to be that St Paul here refers to the Lord's 'knowledge of them that are His' (2 Tim. ii. 19: cp. John x. 27, 28), for time and eternity. All the passages in the Revelation, save iii. 5, are clearly in favour of a reference of the phrase to the certainty of the ultimate salvation of all true saints ... so too Dan. xii. 1 and Luke x. 20. Rev. iii. 5 appears to point in another direction (see Trench on that passage). But in view of the other mentions of the 'Book' in the Revelation the language of iii. 5 may well be only a vivid assertion that the name in question *shall be found* in an indelible register.... Practically, the Apostle here speaks

106

of Clement and the rest as having given illustrious proof of their part and lot in that 'life eternal' which is 'to know the only true God, and Jesus Christ whom He hath sent' (John xvii. 3).—The word *'names'* powerfully suggests the individuality and speciality of divine love." (Note in *The Cambridge Bible for Schools.*)

[8] I think the Apostle has in mind Ps. cxix. 151, where the Septuagint version has *su eggus ei, Kurie.* He is thinking of "the secret *of the Presence*" (Ps. xxxi. 20). We need not shut out the calming thought of the Lord's approaching *Return*; but it does not seem to be the leading thought here.

[9] Bishop Ken.

[10] G. M. Taylor, in *Hymns of Consecration*, 349.

[11] *In the House of the Pilgrimage.*

## THE COLLECTION FOR ST PAUL: THE FAREWELL

"Is thy cruse of comfort wasting? rise and share it with another,
And through all the years of famine it shall serve thee
  and thy brother.

"Is thy burthen hard and heavy? do thy steps drag wearily?
Help to bear thy brother's burthen; God will bear both it and thee.

"Is the heart a living power? self-entwin'd, its strength sinks low;
It can only live in loving, and by serving love will grow."
  E. RUNDLE CHARLES.

# CHAPTER XII

THE COLLECTION FOR ST PAUL: THE FAREWELL

PHILIPPIANS iv. 10-23

The Philippian alms—His sense of their faithful love—He has received in full —A passage in the Scriptural manner—The letter closes—"Christ is preached"—"Together with them"

The work of dictation is nearly done in the Roman lodging. The manuscript will soon be complete, and then soon rolled up and sealed, ready for Epaphroditus; he will place it with reverence and care in his baggage, and see it safe to Philippi.

But one topic has to be handled yet before the end. "Now concerning the collection!" Epaphroditus, who had brought with him to Rome the loving alms of the Philippian believers, must carry back no common thanks to them. All honour shall be done by the Lord's great servant to those who have done the Lord this service in him; they shall know how it has rejoiced and warmed his heart; they shall be made very sure that "inasmuch as they have done it to" their Missionary "they have done it to" their KING.

We do not know how much the money amounted to. It was not improbably a substantial sum. Among the contributors might be Lydia, whose means may well have been comfortable; and the Keeper of the Prison would be by no means a beggar: what gratitude to St Paul glowed in both those hearts! But not in theirs only; the rank and file of the mission would do all that love could do for the man who had manifested JESUS to them. And when that is the spirit, the liberality will often be surprising. Not long ago in one of our North American missions a small meeting of poor Christian Indians apologized for the scantiness of their collection for *missionary objects*; it was worth only £7; they would do better the next time!

But small or large, the Philippian gift was precious with the weight of love. And no doubt it was exceedingly useful practically. It would secure for the imprisoned missionary many alleviating personal comforts, and part of it would probably be spent upon the work of evangelization in Rome and its neighbourhood; for then as now work inevitably meant expense.

Ver. 10. +But+, to turn now from teaching to thanking—+I rejoice+ (*echarên*: the English present best gives the point of the "epistolary" aorist) +in the Lord+, in our union of heart and life with Him, +greatly, that now at length+, after an interval which was no fault of yours, +you have blossomed, out[1]

109

into+ loving +thought on my behalf+. +With a view to this+ (*eph ô*), this effort to aid me, you +were, I know+ (*kai*), +taking thought+ (*ephroneite*), even when you made no sign; +but you were at a loss for opportunity+ for the transmission; no bearer for your bounty could be spared, or found.

Ver. 11. +Not that I speak thus in the tone of need+ (*kath usterêsin*), as if I had been wondering, and fretting, and suspecting you of forgetfulness or of parsimony; no, I have been in a happier mood than that; +for I, for my part+ (*egô*: slightly emphatic), have learnt (*emathon*: our perfect tense best gives this aorist) +to be, in my actual circumstances, self-sufficing+ (*autarkês*); "carrying with me all I have"; independent, not of grace, but of surroundings.

Ver. 12. +I know both+ (*kai*, not *de*) +how to run low,[2] and how to run over+, as I do now, with your bounty; and both experiences need a teaching from above if they are to be rightly borne. +In everything and in all things+, in the details and in the total, I have been let into the secret, I have been initiated into the "mystery,"[3] +of being full fed and of being hungry, of+

Ver. 13. +running over and of coming short. For all things I am strong in Him who makes me able.+[4]

But not even this joyful testimony to the enabling presence of his Lord must divert his thought from the loving act of the Philippians. He seems about to dilate on the glorious theme of what he can be and do in Christ; the wonder of that experience on which he entered at the crisis detailed in 2 Cor. xii. is surely powerfully upon him; the "My grace is sufficient for thee"; the sense of even exultation in weakness and imperfection, "that the power of Christ may overshadow" him. But all this leaves perfectly undisturbed his delicate sympathy with the dear Macedonian converts. And so he will assure them that no spiritual "sufficiency" can blunt the sense of their generous kindness.

Ver. 14. +Yet you did well+, you did a fair, good deed, +when you joined together+ (*sunkoinônêsantes*) +in participating in my tribulation+, with the partnership of a sympathy which feels the suffering it relieves. +But you

Ver. 15. +know+, (to add a thought on your previous bounties, which may as it were correct (*de*) the thought that I needed this last bounty to assure me of your love,) you know, +Philippians,[5] that in the beginning of the Gospel+, in the early days of the mission in your region, +when I left Macedonia+, parting from you on my way south, in order to quit Macedonia (Roman Northern Greece) for Achaia (Roman Southern Greece), *viâ* Thessalonica and Beroea,[6] +no church participated with me+, helped me in my labours, +in the matter of giving and taking+, (they giving and I taking the needed monetary aid,) +but you alone+. But

Ver. 16. you did so; +because even in Thessalonica+; even when I was still there, in a place which was but ninety miles away,[7] and in the same province still; twice over (*kai hapax kai dis*) +you sent+ aid +to my need+, within the few weeks which I spent at Thessalonica.

Again he will not be misunderstood. This warmly expressed gratitude may conceivably be mistaken for an indirect petition, "thanks for favours to come." So with sensitive delicacy he pursues:

Ver. 17. +Not that I am in quest of+ (*epizêtô*: almost, "I am hunting for") +the gift+, the mere sum of money, in and for itself; +but I am in quest of the interest that is accumulating to your account+;[8] I am bent upon just such a developement of your generosity as will win from the heavenly Master more and yet more of that supreme reward, His own "Well done, good and

Ver. 18. faithful." +But+ (he is still anxious, lest this too should be mistaken for a personal bid for more) +I have received in full+ (*apechô*); you have amply discharged love's obligations, in the gift now sent; +and I run over+; the largeness of your bounty makes an overflow. +I have been filled full, in accepting from Epaphroditus what+ came +from you; an odour of fragrancy, a sacrifice acceptable, pleasing to God+, to whom you have really presented what you have sent to the man who serves Him—this evidence of your sacrifice to Him of yourselves and your possessions, a burnt offering (Lev. i. 9) of surrender, a peace offering (Lev. ii. 2, iii. 5) of thanksgiving.[9] I cannot

Ver. 19. requite you; +but my God shall fill up every need of yours+ (*pasan chreian*, not _p.tên chr.*), making up to you in His own loving providence the gap in your means left by this your bounty, and enriching you the while in soul, +according to+, on the scale of, +His wealth, in glory, in Christ Jesus+. Yes, He will draw on no less a treasury than that of "His glory," His own Nature of almighty Love, as it is manifested to and for you "in Christ Jesus," in whom "all the

Ver. 20. Fulness dwells."[10] +But now to our God and Father+, to Him of whom I and you are alike the dear children, +be the glory+, the praise for this and for all like acts of His children's love, +for ever and ever+; "to the ages of the ages," the endless cycles of eternal life, in which shall it be fully seen how He was the Secret of all the holiness of all His saints. *Amen.*

So the utterance of thanks for a loving and liberal collection closes. Here is another case of the phenomenon we have seen already—the beautiful skill with which a local and personal incident is used as the occasion for a whole revelation of grace and truth. We can easily imagine a gift like that which came from Philippi acknowledged with a few cordial words which would adequately express gratitude and pleasure, but would otherwise terminate wholly in themselves. How different is this paragraph! Throughout it, side by side, run at once the most perfect and delicate human courtesy and considerateness, and suggestions of eternal and spiritual relations, in which "the gift" touches at every point the heart of the Lord, and the promises of grace, and the hope of glory. This message of thanks gives us, just in passing, such oracles of blessing as, "I can do all things in Him that strengtheneth me," and "My God shall supply all your need." It is on one side a model of nobility and fineness of human thought and feeling, on the other an oracle of God. This is just in the manner of Scripture. "Never book spake like this Book."

Now the close comes. The greetings which those who are one in the Lord cannot but send to one another in His name, have to be spoken, and then the scribe's pen will rest.

Ver. 21. +Salute every saint in Christ Jesus+, every holy one of your circle, holy because in Him; pass the greetings round from my heart to each member of the Church. And as I write, the Christians now around me, my personal friends upon the spot, must send their message too; +there salute you all the brethren who are with me+. And not they only, but all the believers of the Roman mission, represented around me in my chamber as I dictate, do the same; and among them one class asks to join with special warmth; +there+

Ver. 22. +salute you all the saints, but particularly those who belong to+ (*oi ek*) +the household of the Emperor+ (*kaisaros*); the Christians gathered from the retainers of the Palace; peculiar in their circumstances of temptation, and quickened thereby to a special warmth of faith and love.[11]

Nothing is left now but the final message from the Lord Himself; the invocation of that "grace" which means in fact no abstract somewhat but His living Self, present in His people's inmost being, to vivify and to bless.

Ver. 23. +The grace of our Lord Jesus Christ be with your spirit.[12] Amen.+

The voice is silent; the pen is laid aside. In due time the papyrus roll, inestimable manuscript, is made ready for its journey. And perhaps as it now lies drying the Missionary and his brethren turn to further conversation on the beloved Philippian Church, and recall many a scene in the days that are over, and which are now gliding far into the past of the crowded years; and they speak again of the brightness of Philippian Christian life, and the shadows that lie on it here and there; and then, while the Praetorian sentinel looks on in wonder, or perhaps joins in as a believer, they pray together for Philippi, and pour out their praises to the Father and the Son, and anticipate the day of glory.

It is all over now; it all happened very long ago. But though that blessed group of our elder brethren "are all gone into the world of light" these many more than eighteen hundred human years, that Letter is our contemporary still. "The word of God *liveth* and *abideth for ever*" (1 Pet. i. 23); it is never out of date, never touched by the pathetic glamour of the past, with the suggestion of farewells, and waxings old, and vanishings away. To us to-day, so near the twentieth century, the Epistle to the Philippians is immortal, modern, true for our whole world and time.

And what is its secret, its elixir of undying life? It is the Name of Jesus Christ. It is that these pages are the message of "the chosen Vessel" about that Name.

Our studies in the Epistle shall close with that reflexion. The incidental topics and interests of the document are numerous indeed; but the main theme is one, and it is Jesus Christ. From first to last, under every variety of reference, "Christ is preached."

Let me quote from a Sermon preached many years ago, the last of a series in which I attempted to unfold the Epistle to a Christian congregation in the beloved Church of Fordington, Dorchester, then my Father's cure and charge.

"The mere number of mentions of the Saviour's name is remarkable. More than forty times we have it in this short compass; that is to say, it occurs, amidst all the variety of subjects, on an average of about once in every two or three verses. This is indeed perfectly characteristic, not of this Epistle only but of the whole New Testament. What the Apostles preached was not a thing but a Person; Christ, Christ Jesus, Christ Jesus the Lord.

"But let us not look only on this frequency of mention. Let us gather up something of what these mentions say 'concerning the King.'

"The writer begins with describing himself and his associates as the servants, the absolute bondmen, *of Jesus Christ*. And truly such servants witness to the worthiness of their Master.

"He addresses those to whom he writes as saints, as holy ones, *in Jesus Christ*. Their standing, their character, their all, depends on Him; on union with Him, on life in Him. Without Him, apart from Him, they would not be saints at all.

"The writer speaks of his imprisonment at Rome; the subject is full of Jesus Christ. 'My bonds *in Christ*' is his remarkable description of captivity. And the result of that captivity was, to his exceeding joy, just this, amidst a great variety of conditions in detail, including some exquisite trials to patience and peace: '*Christ* is being preached'; 'that *Christ* may be magnified in my body, whether by life or death.' He is kept absolutely cheerful and at rest; and the secret is Jesus Christ.

"He has occasion to speak of his trial, with its delays, and its suspense between life and death. The whole is full of Jesus Christ. 'To me to live is *Christ*'; He fills, and as it were makes, life for me. 'And to die is gain'—why? Because 'to depart and to be with *Christ* is far, far better.' The dilemma in which he stands (for he is 'in a strait betwixt the two') is a dilemma between Christ and Christ, Christ much and Christ more, Christ by faith and Christ by sight.

"He dwells, in various places, on the life and duties of the Philippians. His precepts are all this, in effect—Christ applied to conduct. 'Let your life-walk be as it becometh the Gospel of *Christ*'; 'Filled with the fruit of righteousness which is through *Jesus Christ*'; 'It is granted to you not only to believe in *Christ* but also to suffer for His sake.'

"In particular, he has to press on them the homely duty of practical self-forgetfulness. He takes them for model and motive to the heaven of heavens, and shews them 'Christ Jesus' there, as for us men and for our salvation He prepares to come down, and comes. 'Let this mind be in you,' as you contemplate the original Glory, the amazing Incarnation, the atoning Death, of *Christ Jesus*.

"He expresses hopes, intentions, resolutions, as to his own actions. All is still 'in Jesus Christ.' 'I trust in *the Lord Jesus* to send Timotheus,' 'I trust in *the Lord* to come myself shortly.'

"Does he speak of the believer's joy? 'We rejoice in *Christ Jesus*,' 'Rejoice in *the Lord* alway, and again I say, Rejoice.' Does he speak of pardon and of peace? 'I counted all things but loss that I might win *Christ*, and be found in Him, having the righteousness which is of God by faith.' Does he speak of knowledge, and of power? 'That I might know *Christ*, and the power of His resurrection, and the fellowship of His sufferings, being made conformable unto His death'; 'I can do all things in *Christ* which strengtheneth me.'

"He speaks of a holy immortality, of eternal glory, and of pleasures for evermore. It is no vague aspiration; it is a sure and certain hope; and it is altogether in Jesus Christ. 'Our home, our citizenship, is in heaven, from whence also we look for the Saviour, the Lord *Jesus Christ*, who shall change the body of our humiliation into likeness to the body of His glory, according to the working whereby He is able even to subdue all things unto—Himself.'

"He bids his beloved converts stand fast; it is 'in *the Lord*.' He bids them be of one mind; it is 'in *the Lord*.' He bids them be always calm, always self-forgetting; '*the Lord* is at hand.' He assures them of an all-sufficient resource for their every need; 'My God shall supply all, according to His riches, in glory, in *Christ Jesus*.'

"His last message of blessing brings together their inmost being and this same wonderful Person; 'The grace of our Lord *Jesus Christ* be with your spirit. Amen.' ...

"What a witness it all is to the glory of our beloved Redeemer; to the majesty of His Person; to the fulness and perfection of His Work; to the solidity, the sobriety, the strength, of the faith which is in Him! There is no inflation or rhetoric in the language of the Epistle about Him. Glowing with love, it is all clear and calm. Yes, for Christ Jesus is not a phantom of the fancy; a hope floating on the thick waves of a wild enthusiasm. He is an anchor, sure and steadfast. Blessed are they who ride secure on the deep, held fast by Him.

"The Epistle witnesses to Him as to a Treasure worth all our seeking, at any cost; infinitely precious to our joyful finding; infinitely deserving of our keeping, of our holding, our 'apprehending,' as He in His mercy has laid hold of us, and will keep hold of us, even to the end; 'unto the day of Jesus Christ.' As then, so now;

'He help'd His saints in ancient days
Who trusted in His name;
And we can witness to His praise,
His love is still the same.'

"May the Spirit bring home to our spirit this great witness of the Epistle; it has its perfect adaptation to each heart, to every life, to every hour.

"Then hereafter we shall give God thanks yet better for 'Philippians,' as we too enter, late or soon, into that world where the Apostle, and Timotheus, and Epaphroditus, and Euodia, and Syntyche, and Clement, and the saints of Caesar's household, have so long beheld the Lord. In that land of light we, who have believed, shall rest with them. We shall know them. In the long leisure of endless life we shall enjoy their company, amidst the multitudinous congregation of the just made perfect. There we shall understand how, under the infinite differences of our earthly conditions, the one Hand led them and led us along the one way of salvation to the one end of everlasting life. Above all, we there, with them, shall know JESUS CHRIST, even as we are known. There we, with them, shall realize how to Him, and to Him alone, from all His servants, from Hebrew, and Roman, and Philippian, and Englishman, and African, from ancients and moderns, wise and ignorant, of all kinds and times, was due the whole praise of their whole salvation.

'Conflicts and trials done
His glory they behold,
Where JESUS and His flock are one,
One Shepherd and one fold.'"

[1] *Anethalete to huper emou phronein.* Literally, "*you shot forth* (as a branch) *thought in my behalf.*" (The English perfect best represents this aorist.) The phrase is unmistakably pictorial, poetical. If I read it aright, it is touched with *a smile* of gentle pleasantry; the warm heart comes out in a not undesigned quaintness of expression.

[2] *tapeinousthai* is used in classical Greek of the falling of a river in drought. Perhaps such an image is present in the language here.

[3] *Memuêmai*: the verb whose root is that of *mysterion, mysterium,* "mystery." In the Greek world "mysteries" were systems of religious belief and practice derived, perhaps, from pre-Hellenic times, and jealously guarded

from common knowledge by their votaries. Admission into their secrets, as into those of Freemasonry now, was sought by people of all kinds, from Roman consuls and emperors downwards; with the special hope of freedom from evil in this life and the next. St Paul's use of this phenomenon to supply language for Christian experience is beautifully suggestive. The knowledge of the peace of God is indeed an *open* secret, open to "whosoever will" "learn of Him." But it is a secret, a mystery, none the less.

*[4]* The word *Christô* should be omitted from the reading, though perfectly right as a note or explanation.—The *iochus* is the forth-putting of the *dunamis* —the *action* of the *faculty.* He is ready to act (or to bear) in a power always latent, always present, through his union with his Lord. The "all things" so met are, of course, the all things of the will of God, the choice of the Master for the servant in the way of circumstance and trial; not the all things of the mere wish or ambition of the servant.

[5] *Philippêsioi*: the Greek form represents a Latin *Philippenses*, by which the residents in the *Roman "colony"* would call themselves. So *Corinthiensis* means not a born Corinthian but a settler at Corinth.—Greek tends to represent a Latin syllable *-ens* by *-ês*: so *Klêmês, Clemens.*

[6] See Acts xvii. 1-15.

[7] On the Egnatian road. He made three stages of the distance; Amphipolis, Apollonia, Thessalonica.

[8] *Ton karpon ton pleonazonta eis logon hymôn.* I venture to render these words as above, as a monetary phrase, relating to principal and interest. It is true that *karpos* is not found used in the sense of interest, for which the regular word is *tokos.* But it would easily fit into the language of the money-market. And St Chrysostom's comment here seems to show that he, a Greek, understood it thus: *horas hoti ekeinois ho karpos tiktetai (tokos).*

[9] For *osmê euôdias* see Eph. v. 2. The phrase is common in the Septuagint to render the Hebrew "savour of rest," the fume of the altar pictorially represented as smelt by the Deity.

[10] This reference of *doxa* seems better than that which would connect it only with the eternal future, the glory of heaven, and make the sentence mean that He would hereafter requite them there. He would indeed do so. But the phrase *plêroun pasan chreian* hardly suggests that thought here.

[11] "Bishop Lightfoot ... (*Philippians*, pp. 171-178) has shewn with great fulness of proof that 'the household of Caesar' was a term embracing a vast number of persons, not only in Rome but in the provinces, all of whom were either actual or former slaves of the Emperor, filling every possible

description of office more or less domestic. The Bishop illustrates his statements from the … burial inscriptions of members of the 'Household' found … near Rome…. These inscriptions afford a curiously large number of coincidences *with the list in Rom. xvi.* … Amplias, Urbanus, Apelles, Tryphaena, Tryphosa, Patrobas, Philologus…. Bishop Lightfoot infers from this whole evidence the great probability that the 'saints' greeted in Rom. xvi. were, on the whole, the same 'saints' who here send greeting *from* Rome…. Their associations and functions, not only in the age of Nero but in the precincts of his court, and probably (for many of them) within the chambers of his palace, give a noble view in passing of the power of grace to triumph over circumstances, and to transfigure life where it seems most impossible" (Note in *The Cambridge Bible for Schools and Colleges*). See also the writer's commentary on the Ep. to the Romans (*Expositor's Bible*), pp. 423-425.

[12] Read *meta tou pneumatos huôn*, not *m. pantôn humôn*.

# THE PRAETORIAN AND THE APOSTLE

ACTS xxviii. 16, 31

"Paul was suffered to dwell by himself with a soldier that kept him.... preaching the kingdom of God, and teaching those things which concern the Lord Jesus Christ."

(THE SOLDIER loquitur.)

Father, the dawn is near! the shield
Of Luna sinks remote and pale
O'er Tiber and the Martial field;
The breeze awakes; the cressets fail:
This livelong night from set of sun
Here have we talk'd: thy task is done.

But yesterday I smil'd or frown'd
To watch thy audience, soon and late,
With scroll and style embattl'd round
In barbarous accents ply debate;
While this would chide, and that would start
Sudden, as sword-struck in the heart.

I laugh'd aside, or, tir'd, withdrew
From the strange sound in waking dreams
To Umbrian hills—the home I knew—
The cottage by Mevania's streams:
'Twas hush'd at length: the guests were flown,
And thou wast left and I alone.

Thou hast forgiven (I know thee now)
The insults of this heathen tongue;
The taunting questions why and how;
The songs (oh madness!) that I sung:
Thou hast forgiv'n the hateful strain
Of dull defiance and disdain.

Thy gaze, thy silence, they compell'd
My own responsive: aw'd I stood
Before thee; soften'd, search'd, and quell'd;
The evil captive to the good:
Half conscious, half entranc'd, I heard
(While the stars mov'd) thy conquering word.

119

These ears were dull to Grecian speech,
This heart more dull to aught but sin;
Yet the great Spirit bade thee reach,
Wake, change, exalt, the soul within:
I've heard; I know; thy Lord, ev'n He,
JESUS, hath look'd from heaven on me.

Thou saw'st me shake, and (spite of pride)
Weep on thy hand: so stern thy truth:
I own'd the terrors that abide
Dread sequel to a rebel's youth:
But soon I pour'd a happier shower
To learn thy Saviour's dying power.

Ah, speechless, rapt, I bent, to know
Each wonder of that fateful day
When midst thy zeal's terrific glow
He met thee on the Syrian way:
I saw, I felt, the scene: my soul
Drank the new bliss, the new control.

Father, the dawn is risen! the hour
Is near, too near, when from this hand
Thy chain must fall—from yonder tower
Another guard must take my stand:
The City stirs: I go, to meet
The foe, the world, in camp and street;

A Christian—yes, for ever now
A Christian: so our Leader keep
My faltering heart: to Him I bow,
His, whether now I wake or sleep:
In peace, in battle, His:—the day
Breaks in the east: oh, once more pray!

1869.